T0322449

SIMPLY CHINESE

BY SUZIE LEE

Photography by
Lizzie Mayson

Recipes from a
Chinese Home Kitchen

Hardie Grant

BOOKS

MEAT 14

SEAFOOD 30

VEGGIES 44

DIM SUM AND DUMPLINGS 58

RICE AND NOODLES 74

ALL-IN-ONE DISHES 88

QUICK MIDWEEK MEALS	98
FAMILY FAVOURITES	112
TAKEAWAYS	130
HONG KONG WESTERN CAFÉ SPECIALS	146
BREAD AND SWEETS	158

170
ABOUT THE AUTHOR

170
ACKNOWLEDGEMENTS

172
INDEX

I am Suzie Lee (Arbuthnot), the 2020 winner of the BBC's *Best Home Cook* and the presenter of my own TV show called *Suzie Lee's Home Cook Heroes* on BBC One. I am British-born Chinese (BBC), and was brought up by my Hong Kong parents in Northern Ireland. My dad moved to Blackburn when he was 11 with his parents to seek a better life. Fast forward seven years and Dad asked Mum to marry him via letter and she travelled to Blackburn to marry him. Fast forward another nine years and I was born (number four of five children).

Tho Man Loo takeaway in Ballymacash was established in 1980 when my parents moved to Lisburn to look for a better life yet again.

Having been brought up with my family running a Chinese takeaway, I was surrounded by food 24/7. In Chinese culture, food and family are intertwined. I was taught that good food can bring harmony and closeness to friends, family and strangers. This is a principle I live by, and I feel when I cook and feed people that I am making a connection with them.

My mum is my inspiration. She was a self-taught cook who ran our takeaway and was our head chef. She loved food and was so passionate about cooking. I am very lucky to have acquired this passion from her. I have such lovely memories of her last year alive, where we went to restaurants, cafés and coffee shops in her very limited spare time to enjoy the delights that Northern Ireland had to offer. If we liked something, we ate it then either she or I would try to recreate it.

The pivotal moment in my cooking life was 25 December, 1999. To my horror, a few days before the holidays, my mum announced she was not going to make Christmas dinner for my extended family. So, I took up the challenge and became familiar with our takeaway industrial oven and gas-fired woks, so I could make dinner for our 40-plus relatives. I love Christmas – it symbolises everything I enjoy about family: time together, food, chatting, laughing and just pure happiness.

Mum unfortunately passed away suddenly on 8 February, 2000. My life was turned upside down and I was propelled into adulthood a lot sooner than I expected. In a strange way I think my mum refusing to cook Christmas dinner the year before was her way of preparing me for the future!

During my 20 years of cooking, I have learned so much through television, magazines, books, my Auntie Linda (my dad's sister) and by experimenting! This meant many different cuisines and ingredients being tried and tested for lots and lots of recipes. Because of this I love a good 'rustle-up' – for me, it goes hand in hand with reducing food waste and using leftovers and what you have at hand in your cupboards, fridge and freezer! I discovered through this writing journey (which was both therapeutic and very emotional) that my mum also 'rustled-up' many a dish and that they were her own original creations.

Cooking Chinese food would not have been my number-1 go-to as I always felt my dishes were not as good as my mum's and auntie's, and this was a real mental hurdle to get over! But in the past seven years since my children were born, I've felt it was so important to bring them up to appreciate and taste their Chinese food heritage too.

Having only had a short period of time with Mum, I was really fortunate to taste amazing traditional Cantonese dishes day in, day out. I was blessed that as a family we travelled a lot and without fail we visited Hong Kong at least once a year. The food there is exceptional! So, with those memories, and having visited many Chinatowns around the world (from all over the UK to New York and Sydney), I feel I am now ready to show you my Chinese cooking repertoire, providing you with recipes that give a different insight into Chinese cooking. Some of these are recreated from memories, some self-taught, some takeaway favourites (like *Cantonese-Style Sweet and Sour Chicken* on page 143) and all have the Suzie twist to them.

My recipes are not restrictive. I believe in using up ingredients you have to hand, so be brave and swap out ingredients for those you already have. The mantra I go by is 'prep, taste and practice'. This will help you become confident in cooking a delicious meal, no matter what it is!

Cooking is meant to be enjoyable and for me it is my therapy and a way to connect with my mum again – I just get lost in the process and go into autopilot as I immerse myself. Now, as a working mum, I am trying to bring my children up to enjoy cooking (playing), eating and communicating through food, whether it is discussing what they are chopping or the simple act of conversation around the table eating the meal that they helped to prepare; food for me is the cornerstone of family life as it brings everyone together.

Go on, give my recipes a try. I promise it really isn't as complicated as it looks.

Enjoy!

SUZIE X

ABOUT THE BOOK

Before, during, and after winning *Best Home Cook* people have always asked for my recipes and top tips in the kitchen. The recipes I have chosen to include in this book are favourites within my small family and can be made by people of all cooking abilities. Cooking should be fun and sharing the results with friends and family makes it all worthwhile.

I was spoilt rotten with all the food that was being cooked around me and my experience of growing up around Chinese cuisine. My Chinese heritage is something I take for granted, and up to now, Chinese cooking was something that I kept within my immediate family. These are memories and my siblings have different ones, but this is my take on some of my mum's dishes to make them even more user-friendly for someone wanting simple, tasty, Cantonese food.

This cookbook is for the home cook and making use of ingredients you can get at your local shop or supermarket; you will only need a few specialist ingredients for some of the dishes. Some of the ingredients might be quite surprising and somewhat unconventional for Hong Kong cuisine – such as tomato ketchup, brown sauce, spam, corned beef, condensed milk, evaporated milk and butter.

I am a big advocate of reducing food waste, so in this book I will give you my top tips on where you can reduce or reuse ingredients to make things go that bit further. My aim is to avoid putting anyone off cooking any of my dishes because they had to buy a million different ingredients that they only used once!

TOP STORECUPBOARD INGREDIENTS

Ginger, garlic and spring onions (scallions) are known as the three key aromatics in Chinese cooking, and they feature heavily throughout my book.

I love spring onions. I have bunches of them sitting in glasses on my kitchen windowsill. They help to lift any dish. You can use the white part to fry with, which gives a similar flavour to onions (although slightly mellower); the green tops are great to give a kick to finished dishes or used raw in salads. The options are endless.

As well as ginger, garlic and spring onions, my other storecupboard staples are listed on the next page. However, you won't find a sprig of coriander (cilantro) in this book, due to a crucial incident in my childhood when I overate it, which has scarred me for life. One of my aunties called by one evening and Mum invited her to stay for dinner. Mum made Cantonese-style steamed turbot, but to finish off the fish (traditionally) a whole bunch of fresh coriander is placed on top of the steaming fish. That evening I decided to eat a gigantic mouthful of coriander with the fish because I was getting praised (as a seven-year-old this meant a lot) for eating everything Mum had made. I gagged (but ate it anyway) and I felt really sick. And that was it – my love affair with coriander was over.

STAPLE INGREDIENTS

FRESH

Root ginger (fresh or frozen)
Onions
Garlic (fresh or frozen)
Spring onions (scallions)
Chillies
Eggs
Vegetables

SEASONING

Light and dark soy sauce
Toasted sesame oil
Oyster sauce or vegetarian
    stir-fry sauce
Shaoxing wine
Rice wine vinegar
Black sesame oil

Dried fermented black beans
Brown sauce
Ground bean sauce
Chilli oil
Black vinegar
Sesame paste
Peanut butter
Vegetable oil
Fine sea salt
White pepper
Black pepper
Sesame oil
Chinese five spice powder
    (cinnamon, cloves, fennel,
    star anise, Szechuan
    peppercorns)
Chicken or veg bouillon/
    powder
Caster (superfine) and
    granulated sugar
Stock cubes

DRY (BACK UP)

Onion powder/granules
Garlic powder/granules
Chilli powder/flakes
Ground ginger
Dried shiitake mushrooms
Sesame seeds
    (white, black or both)
Peanuts
Wood ear mushrooms
Dried lily flowers

OTHER

Basmati rice
Noodles – rice, egg, glass
Cornflour (cornstarch)
Rice flour
Plain flour
Wheat starch
Spam/corned beef
Wonton wrappers

MUST-HAVE EQUIPMENT

There are a couple of must-have items which will aid you on this *Simply Chinese* cooking journey, and therefore I feel are worth the investment.

WOK

You do not have to buy an expensive non-stick wok. The key to making a stainless-steel, aluminium or cast-iron wok non-stick is to 'season it'. To do this, use some paper towel to rub vegetable or sunflower oil over the inside of the wok, so the whole surface has a light coating of oil. Heat the wok slowly on the stovetop until it is smoking and then wipe thoroughly with more paper towel. Repeat the oiling, heating and wiping process until the paper towel comes away clean. The wok will blacken and lose its silver colour. It is now seasoned and you have given your wok 'wok hay', which means 'energy or breath of the wok'.

SIEVE

Use to strain noodles, blanch vegetables and remove excess food fragments from oil if deep-frying.

STEAMER

Steamer, or a large pan with a lid into which you can fit a trivet stand, steam rack and heatproof dish.

TONGS

Used to extract food from woks and pots and to mix and stir.

MEASURING JUG, SPOONS AND SCALES

These items are important for the precision required in the recipes.

KEY TERMS AND TIPS

You will find that I use some methods, terms and ingredients frequently throughout the book and I thought it would be helpful to pull them all together and explain them fully here.

CORNFLOUR (CORNSTARCH)

A versatile ingredient that can be used in the following ways:

- Velveting – adding cornflour to your meat marinade. As the meat cooks, the cornflour acts as a barrier, helping to keep moisture in and the meat juicy.

- Binding ingredients together in recipes such as the *Deep-fried Fish Cakes* on page 37 and wontons in the *Homemade Wonton Soup Noodles* (page 78).

- Crisping – used to help form a crispy exterior when deep- or pan-frying foods (see *Cantonese-Style Sweet and Sour Chicken* on page 143).

- Noodles – giving them a slightly translucent quality. See my *Cheung Fun* and *Ho Fun Noodle* recipes on pages 81 and 114, respectively.

- Thickener – use it to create a paste for thickening soups and sauces. Cornflour paste is the key sauce thickener in all Chinese cooking. It is made by combining cornflour and water at a ratio of 1:2. Mix together 1 tablespoon of cold or cooled water and 1 tablespoon of cornflour in a bowl until fully combined. Do not use hot water as this will create a lumpy mixture. Remember to give the mixture a stir before using, as the cornflour will have settled to the bottom of the bowl.

BLANCHING/PARBOILING MEAT

This is always done in Chinese cooking. Put your meat in a pan of cold water and bring it up to the boil to allow the impurities to float to the surface. This helps reduce excess fat in the meat, removes blood from the bones and the taste of gaminess from the meat, which it might add to the dish and ensures the broth or soup you are making with the meat will be very clear. I hate waste so I don't actually throw away the water the meat was boiled in as it holds a lot of flavour. I just make sure the impurities and scum are scooped away with a sieve from the surface of the liquid.

STEAMING

This is a big part of my book. It is a great way to cook vegetables to retain their nutrients, and to steam meat and dumplings. So, if you do not have a steamer, I would highly recommend getting one!

SPLASH OF WATER

Always add a splash of water to vegetables when stir-frying to stop them from catching and burning in the wok.

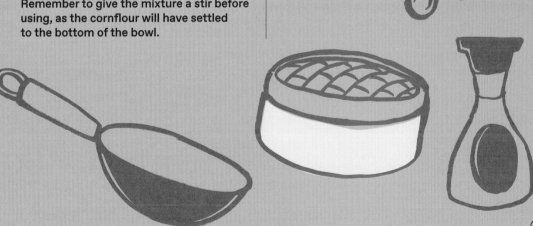

DOUGHS

Many of the doughs for the pancake, spring roll and wonton wrappers, dim sum, dumplings and noodles can be shop-bought, but if you would like to try making them from scratch, follow the recipes here.

PANCAKE WRAPPERS

plain (all-purpose) flour,
    plus extra for dusting .... 200 g (7 oz/1⅔ cups)
salt..large pinch
oil, plus extra for oiling
    the pancakes.................................1 teaspoon
boiling water................200 ml (7 fl oz/scant 1 cup)

Put the flour, salt and oil in a large heatproof mixing bowl. Pour in the boiling water and mix with chopsticks or a wooden spoon until a dough is formed. Cover the bowl with a damp tea towel or cling film (plastic wrap) and leave for 10 minutes – this helps to develop the gluten and makes the dough easier to knead.

Knead the dough on a work surface dusted with flour for about 5 minutes until smooth. Return to the bowl, cover again and let it rest for about 15 minutes.

Divide the dough into 16 equal portions. Take one portion of dough, brush a little oil on the surface and press another portion on top. Dust a piece of baking parchment with flour, place the doubled-up dough on top and roll the two pieces together to form a 10 cm (4 in) disc. It should be nice and thin.

WRAPPER DOUGH

wheat starch..........................50 g (1¾ oz/ ⅓ cup)
cornflour (cornstarch)...........50 g (1¾ oz/ ⅓ cup)
salt..pinch
vegetable oil, plus extra
    for oiling the rolling pin............2½ teaspoons

Put the wheat starch, cornflour and salt in a heatproof bowl. Slowly add 100 ml (3½ fl oz/ scant ½ cup) of boiling water and mix quickly with a wooden spoon to form a dough. Add the oil and mix until combined. Put on a pair of rubber gloves and, once the dough is cool enough to touch, knead the dough in the bowl until it forms a smooth ball.

Divide the dough evenly into 16 pieces and lightly oil a rolling pin with your hand. Roll each piece into a smooth circle, 10 cm (4 in) in diameter and roughly 2 mm (1/16 in) thick. Keep the rolled-out pieces of dough under a damp cloth until you are ready to use them.

DONUT DOUGH

large egg...1
self-raising flour, plus extra
    for rolling....................200 g (7 oz/1⅔ cup)
bicarbonate of soda (baking soda) .... ⅛ teaspoon
salt...¼ teaspoon
vegetable oil, plus extra
    for greasing.............................1 tablespoon

Crack the egg into a bowl or jug on digital scales, then make up the weight to 125 g (4½ oz) with warm water. Put the egg and water mixture in a bowl and add the flour, bicarbonate of soda, salt and oil. Mix until combined, then cover and leave for 10 minutes. This step is called 'autolysing': it helps to develop the gluten and cuts down the kneading time. After 10 minutes, knead the dough on a work surface dusted with flour for about 5 minutes until smooth (or use a stand mixer fitted with the dough hook). Grease the bowl the dough was mixed in lightly with oil, then shape it into a ball, place it in the bowl and cover with cling film (plastic wrap). Place in the oven with just the light on or in a warm place, for 1 hour so the dough can prove and relax.

To make the donut sticks, halve the dough and place both pieces onto a flour-dusted work surface. Lightly roll them into two long rectangular strips about 25 x 6 cm (10 x 2½ in). Cut about ten 2.5 cm (1 in) pieces from each strip. Stick one piece of dough on top of another and use a chopstick to press it down the middle lengthways, so the top rectangle sticks to the bottom one.

GYOZA WRAPPER DOUGH

plain (all-purpose) flour..........120 g (4¼ oz/1 cup)
strong bread flour...............60 g (2¼ oz/ ½ cup)
plain flour..........................60 g (2¼ oz/ ½ cup)
salt..½ teaspoon
cornflour (cornstarch), for dusting

Put the flours and salt in a heatproof bowl, add 120–160 ml (4–5½ fl oz/½–⅔ cup) of boiling water and, with rubber gloves, knead for a couple of minutes to make a rough dough. Divide into four logs, wrap each one in cling film (plastic wrap) or beeswax wrap and rest for 1 hour at room temperature.

Dust a work surface with cornflour. Cut each log into 10 evenly-sized balls of dough and roll each piece into an 8 cm (3 in) disc no more than 2 mm (1/16 in) thick – the thinner the better, otherwise the wrappers will be too chewy (you can tidy up the edges with a pastry cutter or mug). Dust well with cornflour. Cover with cling film and put in the fridge.

BAOZI DOUGH

granulated sugar	8 g (1/4 oz)
sachet of fast-action dried yeast	7 g (1/4 oz)
plain (all-purpose) flour, plus extra for dusting	200 g (7 oz/1⅓ cup)
baking powder	½ teaspoon
vegetable oil, plus extra for greasing	1 teaspoon

Put 100 ml (3½ fl oz/scant ½ cup) of lukewarm water and the sugar in a bowl and stir to dissolve the sugar, then stir in the yeast and set aside for 5 minutes until the yeast starts to 'bloom' (the surface will go foamy, which means the yeast is working). Add the flour, baking powder and oil and mix with a wooden spoon until the dough is roughly combined. Cover with a damp tea towel and leave the dough to rest for 5 minutes, then knead for about 5 minutes, or until the dough is smooth. Lightly grease a bowl, pop in the dough, cover with a plate or cling film (plastic wrap), then put in an oven with just the light on (not set to a temperature) or in a warm place for about 30 minutes, until doubled in size.

Divide the dough into 12 pieces, roughly 25 g (1 oz) each, then roll each piece into a tight ball, tucking the edges underneath (this helps create tension on the surface of the dough, which helps it hold its shape). Roll each ball flat on a floured surface with a rolling pin to make circles with a thickness of 4–5 mm (¼ in).

BAO BUNS

granulated sugar	1 tablespoon
sachets of fast-action dried yeast	2 x 14 g (½ oz)
plain (all-purpose) flour	375 g (13 oz/3 cups)
vegetable oil	1 teaspoon

To make the bao dough, put 175 ml (6 fl oz/¾ cup) of lukewarm water in a bowl, add the sugar, stir to dissolve, then add the yeast and leave for 5 minutes until it starts to foam. Mix the ingredients together with a wooden spoon until roughly combined. Then put the dough back in the bowl, cover with cling film (plastic wrap) and keep in a warm place (such as the oven with just the light on) for 30 minutes until it has doubled in size.

When ready, knead the dough for a couple of minutes on a floured surface, then cut it into 16 pieces and roll each of these into an oblong of dough – brush with vegetable oil on both sides then fold over.

EGG NOODLES AND WONTON WRAPPERS

strong white bread flour	450 g (1 lb/3½ cups)
egg and hot water mixture (3 eggs, plus enough hot water to make up to the weight required)	250 g (9 oz)
salt	½ teaspoon
kai sun (baked bicarbonate of soda /baking soda or lye water)	1 teaspoon
cornflour (cornstarch), for dusting	

Pulse the bread flour, eggs, salt and *kai sun* in a food processor until crumbly in texture. Then knead, until it comes into a ball. Cover with cling film (plastic wrap) or a damp tea towel and leave for 10 minutes.

After 10 minutes, divide the dough into manageable chunks – roughly six to eight balls.

Using a pasta machine, go from the thickest setting to the thinnest to roll out each piece of dough. Use cornflour to stop the pastry sticking together. You want the pastry to be about 2 mm (1/16 in) thick. If you do not have a pasta machine, then use a rolling pin to roll the dough to a 2 mm thickness.

Make approximately 32 square wrappers, then stack and dust each one with cornflour. Put the leftover dough through the pasta maker to make approximately four nests of noodles. If you're not using a pasta machine, use a sharp knife to cut the dough into noodles. Make sure you store the wrappers and noodles under a damp tea towel if you are not using them straight away.

SPRING ROLL WRAPPER

plain (all-purpose) flour, plus extra to
    make a paste.................250g (9 oz/2 cups)
salt...½ teaspoon

To make the spring roll wrappers, mix the flour and salt in a bowl with 375 ml (13 fl oz/1⅔ cup) of cold water and whisk together, then pour through a sieve into another bowl. Place a non-stick frying pan (skillet) over the lowest heat for at least 5 minutes, then, using a pastry brush, brush the mixture all over the hot, dry pan until the pan surface is covered. Increase the heat for about 30 seconds until the sheet turns white, then remove the wrapper from the pan and place it in a damp tea towel to stop it from drying out. Wipe the pan clean with a damp cloth and repeat the process until all the mixture has been used up. The mixture should make about 12–14 wrappers.

BREAD DOUGH

YEAST
yeast...8 g (⅓ oz)
lukewarm milk, plus extra for brushing..... 125 ml
    (4¼ fl oz/generous ½ cup)

ROUX
plain flour...............................2½ tablespoons
whole milk.......................65 ml (2 fl oz/¼ cup)
water.................55 ml (1¾ fl oz/3½ tablespoons)

DOUGH
plain (all-purpose) flour....350 g (12 oz/2¾ cups)
caster (superfine)
    sugar....................35 g (1¼ oz/3 tablespoons)
salt..3 g
medium egg...1
condensed milk........40 g (1½ oz/2 tablespoons)
butter, melted, plus extra
    for greasing...........................60 g (2¼ oz)

Put the yeast in the lukewarm milk and stir it in so it 'blooms' (the surface will go foamy which means the yeast is working).

Combine all the ingredients for the roux in a

microwave-safe cup to form a paste, then heat in the microwave for 10 seconds and stir twice. Alternatively, combine them in a saucepan over a low heat for 10 minutes until thickened and custard-like.

To make the dough, mix the roux with the flour, sugar, salt, egg, condensed milk and the yeast mixture in a stand mixer fitted with a dough hook for 3–5 minutes until well combined, then add the melted butter while the mixer is still running and mix until the butter is completely incorporated. Alternatively, mix the ingredients in a bowl using an electric whisk with dough hooks or knead with your hands to combine. Leave the dough to rest for 20 minutes at room temperature, covered with a damp tea towel.

Knead the rested dough for 5 minutes (by hand or with the electric whisk or stand mixer at medium speed), then shape the dough into a ball, tucking the dough under at the bottom so the surface is nice and smooth. Put it back in the bowl, cover and leave in an oven with just the light on (not set to a temperature) for 30 minutes until it has doubled in size.

BUTTER CRUMB AND WATER PASTRY

BUTTER CRUMB
plain (all-purpose) flour.....100 g (3½ oz/ ¾ cup)
frozen butter, grated.......................150 g (5 oz)

WATER PASTRY
plain (all-purpose) flour.....200 g (7 oz/1⅔ cups)
icing (confectioner's) sugar,
    sifted...............50 g (1¾ oz/generous ⅓ cup)
small egg...1
vegetable oil, for greasing

To make the butter crumb, toss the flour and grated butter together in a bowl and mix well – the mixture should have a floury, lumpy texture.

Put the flour and icing sugar in a food processor and pulse to combine, then add the egg and pulse again, and finally add 1 teaspoon of ice-cold water at a time and pulse after each addition until you have a crumbly dough mixture (you will need about 60 ml/2 fl oz/¼ cup) – you do not want it to be smooth; if it's smooth, that means you have added too much water. Place a large piece of cling film (plastic wrap) on your work surface, lightly grease it with oil, then place the water pastry on top. Lightly oil the top of the pastry, then place another piece of cling film on top. Roll into a large 2-mm (1/16-in) thick rectangle between the two layers of cling film. Remove the top layer of cling film and rotate the rectangle so a long side is parallel to you (with the pastry still on the cling film), and imagine the rectangle is spilt into thirds. Put half of the butter crumb mixture on two-thirds of the water pastry, then fold the non-covered third of the pastry over the middle third. Fold the last exposed third of pastry with butter crumb on top of the other middle third. Be careful the butter crumb does not spill out of the pastry. Rotate the dough 90 degrees

and, using the rolling pin, roll it out to a long rectangle again. Repeat the folding and rolling step again with the remaining half of the butter and crumb mixture (this is your second folding stage). Repeat the 90-degree rotation, folding into thirds and rolling a further three times – this builds up the lamination layers – to get flaky pastry. (If at any stage the butter starts to leak out, wrap it up and put into the fridge to firm up for another 10 minutes and then carry on with the folds.) Cover the dough (which is now a thick smaller rectangle) with cling film and chill in the fridge for at least 20 minutes.

MEAT

I am a self-confessed carnivore and everyone in my family loves protein-packed meals. Here, I've included some restaurant classics as well as my favourites. The Chinese believe meat is of high importance to your diet. Back in the 1950s and 60s, it was a luxury to be able to afford meat and it was therefore deemed to be highly nutritious.

CHAPTER ONE

CRISPY PORK BELLY	16
DUCK PANCAKES	18
SOY SAUCE CHICKEN	20
SUZIE'S CHINESE FRIED CHICKEN	22
PEKING PORK CHOPS	25
HAINANESE CHICKEN RICE	26
GRANDAD'S SPECIAL STEAK	28

Crispy Pork Belly

Crispy Pork Belly (*siu yuk*) is a very popular roasted Chinese meat dish. It is usually served with rice or noodles, but can also be used as the filling for bao buns. Crispy Pork Belly is a dish that my family always orders when we go to a Chinese restaurant – it brings back so many memories. Pork belly is a thrifty cut of meat, and this dish can feed a lot of people.

Serves: 6
Prep: 15 minutes, plus chilling overnight
Cook: 2 hours 20 mins

INGREDIENTS

pork belly with skin .... 1 kg (2 lb 4 oz)
sea salt .... about 400 g (14 oz)
Chinese five-spice powder .... 2 tablespoons
white pepper .... large pinch

METHOD

Pat the pork belly dry on all sides with paper towel, then use a skewer, toothpick or sharp knife to pierce the skin as many times as you can, being careful to avoid piercing the flesh. Place on a grill rack in a shallow roasting tin (pan) skin side up, so the flesh is not touching the bottom of the tin, then cover the skin with a thick layer of about 200 g (7 oz) of the salt (this may seem excessive, but it draws out the moisture in the skin to give you the crispiest pork belly ever). You are aiming for a 3-mm (⅛-in) thick layer of salt. Put the pork in the roasting tin, uncovered, on the bottom shelf of the fridge or the meat drawer and leave overnight.

The next day, preheat the oven to 130°C fan (300°F/gas 2).

Take the pork out of the fridge and scrape all the salt off the skin. Pat the pork dry with paper towel. Flip the pork, skin side down, onto a chopping board and massage the Chinese five-spice and white pepper all over the flesh, trying to avoid covering the skin with this rub.

Put the pork belly on a sheet of heavy-duty foil – it should fully contain the belly with a 2.5 cm (1 in) rim up the sides. Make sure the foil is tightly encasing the sides of the meat. Pierce the skin again (don't pierce through to the flesh), then add the rest of the salt to cover the top and edges, so it acts as a seal: this will help the pork belly steam from underneath and the fat will render and soften further and become more melt in the mouth.

Roast the pork belly in the oven for 2 hours.

Take the pork out of the oven and increase the temperature to 220°C fan (475°F/gas 9).

TOP TIP

Use any leftover pork belly in the *Sticky Pork Belly Bao Buns* (see page 72), any stir-fry dishes or serve with rice or noodle bowls.

Carefully remove the pork from the foil, making sure none of the salt gets into the juices that have accumulated in the foil. These juices are delicious – don't throw them out as they can be used to flavour other dishes. I love tossing them into noodle bowls and they also give an extra layer of flavour to steamed vegetables. Flake off all the salt from the pork using a pastry brush and paper towel. Pat the skin dry with paper towel, then place the pork on a smaller baking tray (pan), skin side up, and return to the oven for 15–20 minutes until the skin has puffed up.

Remove the pork belly from the oven and leave it to rest and cool for about 5 minutes, then use a super-sharp knife to chop it into cubes.

Duck Pancakes

Duck is one of my favourite meats and Duck Pancakes is a great sharing dish – or just a large meal for yourself if you're feeling really hungry! For this recipe I like to use duck legs as I think they have more flavour, but feel free to use breast if you prefer.

Serves: 4
Prep: 10 minutes
Cook: 1 hour 40 minutes

INGREDIENTS

DUCK

Chinese five-spice powder .... 4 teaspoons
hoisin sauce .... 4 teaspoons
duck legs (or breasts) 4
piece of fresh root ginger, sliced ..... 40 g (1½ oz)
spring onions
    (scallions) .... 70 g (2½ oz) [about 4]
vegetable oil, for brushing
salt and white pepper

PANCAKES

shop-bought pancakes (or see the
    Pancake Wrapper recipe on page 10) 8

TO SERVE

spring onions (scallions), thinly sliced
    lengthways 4
hoisin sauce
cucumber, sliced into thin batons (remove the
    watery seeds if you are not eating them
    straight away or it will make everything
    soggy!) 1

METHOD

Preheat the oven to 160°C fan (350°F/gas 4).

Rub 1 teaspoon of Chinese five-spice powder and 1 teaspoon of hoisin sauce into each duck leg or breast, rubbing them into the exposed flesh. Put the ginger and spring onions in a shallow roasting tin (pan) with grill rack and pour over enough water to cover the bottom (about 250 ml/8½ fl oz/1 cup). Put the grill rack in the roasting tin. Place the duck on the grill rack, making sure it isn't touching the water, and brush with a little vegetable oil. Sprinkle with salt and pepper, cover the whole roasting tin with foil and bake the duck in the oven for at least 1 hour 30 minutes until tender.

While the duck is in the oven, and if you are making these from scratch, prepare the pancakes following the instructions on page 10.

Brush a frying pan (skillet) with a little oil and place over a medium heat. Add a pancake and fry for 30–60 seconds until one side is dotted with brown circles. Turn the pancake over and cook for another 30–60 seconds. Carefully remove the pancake from the pan and, if you have made the pancakes from scratch, peel the two pieces apart while still warm. Put the two separated pancakes back in the pan for about 30 seconds – too long and they will turn into crisps! Place the pancakes on a plate under a slightly damp tea towel to keep them soft and warm. Repeat with the rest of the dough.

Place the sliced spring onions in a bowl of cold water to refresh them. Remove the duck from the oven and shred the meat off the bones. If the meat seems slightly dry (this might be the case if you've used breast meat), add a little bit of the liquid sitting at the bottom of the roasting tin and mix it through the meat.

Serve the shredded duck with the pancakes, hoisin sauce, drained spring onions and cucumber.

TOP TIPS

Both the meat and the pancakes can be made in advance and frozen for future use.

Use any leftover duck for the *Duck and Pineapple Fried Rice* (see page 86).

Soy Sauce Chicken

Chicken is very popular in Cantonese cooking; it is cooked in so many ways that it would take me months to write up the recipes! This chicken dish is a must on so many levels. It is easy to make and it has a great sauce, which you can use elsewhere. I have simplified the recipe even further by cutting the chicken into pieces, which ensures an even colour. Serve with rice.

Serves: 4
Prep: 5 minutes
Cook: 35 minutes, plus resting and cooling

INGREDIENTS

whole chicken, chopped into 6 sections
(2 breasts, bone-in, 2 legs and
2 wings) .... 1.3–1.5 kg (3–3 lb 5 oz)
or chicken legs .... 1 kg (2 lb 4 oz)

SAUCE

vegetable oil .... 1 tablespoon
piece of fresh ginger root,
thinly sliced .... 40 g (1½ oz)
spring onions (scallions), cut into 5 cm (2 in)
lengths and smashed 3
star anise 4
Shaoxing wine .... 300 ml (10 fl oz/1¼ cups)
light soy sauce .... 300 ml (10 fl oz/1¼ cups)
dark soy sauce .... 200 ml (7 fl oz/scant 1 cup)
caster (superfine) sugar .... 225 g (8 oz/1 cup)
salt .... 10 g (¼ oz)

METHOD

First, make the sauce. Heat the oil in a large saucepan over a high heat, add the ginger, spring onions and star anise and fry for about 5 minutes until softened. Add the Shaoxing wine, soy sauces, sugar and salt. Bring to the boil, then reduce the heat and simmer for 10 minutes.

Put the chicken pieces in the same saucepan, skin side down, and cook for 20–25 minutes. Ideally, they should be fully submerged in the sauce – if they aren't, baste them now and again with the sauce. Turn off the heat and let the chicken sit in the liquid for 15 minutes – this helps give the chicken skin that famous brown soy-sauce colour.

Take the chicken pieces out of the liquid and leave to cool for at least 15 minutes (this makes it much easier to cut the meat). Use a sharp knife to cut the meat into chunks, leaving the bones intact, place on a dish and spoon over some of the dark rich sauce.

TOP TIPS

If you want to save time without compromising on taste, use mini chicken fillets and cook in the sauce for 10–12 minutes.

I use the leftover sauce instead of soy sauce when making fried rice and often turn to it as a marinade for chicken wings, too.

Suzie's Chinese Fried Chicken

A very well-known deep-fried chicken chain was my sneaky go-to when I was pregnant. The crunchy, tasty exterior and tender chicken was just to die for! So, I created my own Chinese-flavoured, shallow-fried version. These crispy chunks of chicken are delicious served between a burger bap or alongside a salad!

Serves: 4
Prep: 15 minutes, plus 15 minutes marinating time
Cook: 20 minutes

INGREDIENTS

skinless and boneless
    chicken thighs .... about 600 g (1 lb 5 oz)
    [about 6 thighs]
vegetable oil, for frying .... 300–500 ml
    (10–17 fl oz/1¼–2 cups)

MARINADE

dark soy sauce .... 1 tablespoon
grated fresh ginger root .... 1 tablespoon
crushed garlic .... 2 teaspoons
toasted sesame oil .... 1 teaspoon
cornflour (cornstarch) .... 1 teaspoon
salt .... pinch
white pepper .... ½ teaspoon
small egg 1

FLOUR MIX

cornflour (cornstarch) .... 75 g (2½ oz/¾ cup)
plain (all-purpose) flour .... 75 g (2½ oz/
    scant ½ cup)
Chinese five-spice powder .... 2 teaspoons
garlic powder .... 2 teaspoons
ground ginger .... 2 teaspoons
white pepper .... ¼ teaspoon
salt .... ¼ teaspoon

METHOD

Preheat the oven to 160°C fan (350°F/gas 4) and line a grill tray or baking tray (pan) with foil.

Put the marinade ingredients in a bowl or resealable food bag and combine well. Add the chicken thighs, coat them in the marinade and let them marinate for at least 15 minutes (you can leave them in the fridge marinating overnight and they will be so full of flavour).

Put the flour mix ingredients in a large bowl and mix everything together with a fork.

Heat the vegetable oil in a large wok or pan for shallow-frying the chicken – you want enough oil to fill the pan to a depth of 1.5 cm (⅝ in). Set the wok or pan over the highest heat. To test if the oil is ready, place the end of a wooden spoon into the hot oil: bubbles should fizz around it straight away. If the oil is smoking, it is too hot and you should reduce the temperature.

While the oil is heating up, coat the marinated chicken thighs. Put a piece of chicken in the flour mix and make sure it is completely coated. Shake off any excess flour mixture. Repeat for each piece.

Carefully lower two pieces of coated chicken into the hot oil and cook for 4–5 minutes until one side is crispy and golden, then use tongs to flip the chicken and fry on the other side for 4–5 minutes.

Carefully remove the chicken from the hot oil with tongs and place on the lined tray. Fry the rest of the chicken, then put into the oven to crisp up further for 10 minutes. Then it is ready to serve.

TOP TIP

Do not throw out the oil you used for frying the chicken. Instead, wait until it has cooled, then place a piece of paper towel inside a funnel and put this in the mouth of a glass bottle. In small batches, strain the oil into the bottle. I use my oil about three times before it gets too dark, burned or tinged with flavours from previous dishes.

Peking Pork Chops

Peking Pork Chops are a firm favourite in my household. My Auntie Linda would make these quite often at big family events and they were always one of the first dishes to be cleared! Really, the sauce is so tasty that you can use any meat or veg as an alternative to pork.

Serves: 4
Prep: 10 minutes, plus 5 minutes' marinating time
Cook: 15 minutes

INGREDIENTS

pork chops, trimmed of fat ... about 400 g (14 oz)
vegetable oil .... about 200 ml
    (7 fl oz/scant 1 cup)
cornflour (cornstarch) .... 2 tablespoons
plain (all-purpose) flour .... 2 tablespoons
spring onions (scallions), sliced, to garnish

MARINADE

Shaoxing wine .... 1½ tablespoons
light soy sauce .... 1½ tablespoons
Chinese five-spice powder .... ¼ teaspoon
cornflour (cornstarch) .... 1 teaspoon
toasted sesame oil .... 1 teaspoon
small egg 1

SAUCE

tomato ketchup .... 3 tablespoons
chilli oil (see my recipe for *Spicy Crispy
    Tofu Bites with Suzie's Chilli Oil*
    on page 48 or use a chilli oil you
    have to hand) .... ½ teaspoon
hoisin sauce .... 3 tablespoons
Worcestershire sauce .... 3 tablespoons
granulated sugar .... 1 teaspoon
salt .... ¼ teaspoon
Chinese five-spice powder .... 2 teaspoons

METHOD

Use a mallet to bash both sides of the pork chops so they are thinner (this tenderises the meat, too), then cut each chop into three or four large chunks.

Put the marinade ingredients in a bowl and mix well with a fork. Add the tenderised pork chop pieces and toss to coat. Cover with foil or cling film (plastic wrap) and leave to marinate for at least 5 minutes, or you can leave them covered in the refrigerator overnight.

Heat the vegetable oil in a wok or frying pan (skillet) over a high heat – you want enough to cover the bottom of the wok or pan. To test if the oil is ready, place the end of a wooden spoon into the hot oil: bubbles should fizz around it straight away. If the oil is smoking, it is too hot and you should reduce the temperature.

While the oil is heating up, coat the pork chops. Combine the cornflour and flour in a bowl, then add to the marinated pork pieces and toss – try to coat each piece lightly but evenly. Carefully drop a few pieces of pork into the hot oil (fry them in batches, to avoid overcrowding the wok or pan) and fry for a couple of minutes on each side until crispy, turning them with tongs. Transfer to paper towel to absorb any excess oil.

Put the sauce ingredients in a separate a wok or frying pan with 3 tablespoons of water and let it bubble away for about 5 minutes until it becomes thick and sticky. Taste and season accordingly.

Toss your fried pork pieces in the sauce and cook for another couple of minutes. Plate up and garnish with spring onions and serve with boiled rice.

Hainanese Chicken Rice

Hainanese chicken originates from the province of Hainan in Southwest China and it has made its way to Hong Kong, Singapore, Malaysia and Thailand. Each country has its own take on this dish, but the chicken is always poached. Mum started to make a simplified version of this dish a couple of years before she passed away, and this is the recipe I share with you here.

Serves: 4
Prep: 20 minutes
Cook: 1 hour

INGREDIENTS

CHICKEN

whole chicken, fat trimmed
  and set aside .... 1.3–1.5 kg (3–3 lb 5 oz)
piece of fresh ginger root,
  thinly sliced .... 50 g (1¾ oz)
large spring onions (scallions),
  roughly chopped 2
large garlic cloves, smashed 4
sea salt .... 1 teaspoon
chicken stock powder or ½ chicken
  stock cube (optional) .... 1 teaspoon
spring onions (scallions), thinly sliced, to garnish

RICE

vegetable oil .... 1 teaspoon
small onion, finely diced 1
grated fresh ginger root .... 1 tablespoon
grated garlic .... 1 teaspoon
basmati rice, rinsed in cold water
  and drained .... 400 g (14 oz/2 cups)

GINGER AND SPRING ONION SAUCE

piece of fresh ginger root,
  finely chopped .... 30 g (1 oz)
spring onions (scallions),
  finely chopped .... 60 g (2¼ oz)
sea salt .... 1 teaspoon
vegetable oil .... 90 ml (3 fl oz/6 tablespoons)

TOP TIP

If you want to make this simpler, use 1.3–1.5 kg (3–3 lb 5 oz) of chicken thighs or legs.

METHOD

Cut off any excess skin from the chicken and reserve it for frying with the rice later.

Bring a large saucepan of water to the boil (enough for the chicken to be submerged in). Add the chicken to the pan (breast side down) and bring to the boil, then simmer for 5 minutes, scooping off any scum from the surface.

Add the ginger, spring onions, garlic, salt and chicken stock powder or crumbled stock cube (if using) to the pan and simmer over a medium heat for 30–35 minutes until the chicken is cooked. Carefully lift out the chicken and let it cool, retaining the poaching broth. Once cooled, chop the chicken into chunks with a sharp knife or cleaver.

Heat the vegetable oil for the rice in a saucepan over a high heat. Add the chicken skin trimmings and fry until crispy, then add the onion, ginger and garlic and toss in the drained rice. Mix until the rice is coated. Add four ladles of the chicken stock from the poaching broth – bring to a simmer and once the water has been absorbed, repeat with more ladles of stock until the rice is cooked. You should need about 600 ml (20 fl oz/2½ cups) of poaching liquid and it should take about 20 minutes; you do not want to make the rice sticky, so avoid stirring it too much. Cover to keep the rice warm and steaming.

To make the sauce, mix the ginger, spring onions and salt in a heatproof bowl. Bring the vegetable oil to the boil in a small flameproof pot – you will see the surface rippling and that is when it is at boiling point – or you can test with the end of the wooden spoon: bubbles will fizz around a wooden spoon immediately. Pour this boiling-hot oil over the bowl of ginger and spring onion.

Plate everything up and serve.

Grandad's Special Steak

My dad can cook, but I don't think I really realised this until my mum passed away. He started to make this dish quite frequently – I have always called it his special steak dish but it was actually his dad's! Dad makes his version with whole steaks, but cooking steak to everyone's liking is tricky so I have simplified it by thinly slicing and flash-frying the meat. It is a very tangy dish (the key ingredients being brown sauce and Worcestershire sauce) and goes so well with rice. Oh! And the onions are just something else!

Serves: 4
Prep: 5 minutes
Cook: 15 minutes

INGREDIENTS

STEAK

rump steak, thinly sliced on the diagonal
    to create flat, thin and
    broad pieces .... about 400 g (14 oz)
dark soy sauce .... 1 tablespoon
cornflour (cornstarch) .... 1 teaspoon
vegetable oil .... 2 tablespoons

SAUCE

vegetable oil .... 1 teaspoon
large onion, thickly sliced 1
brown sauce .... 6 generous tablespoons
Worcestershire sauce .... 3 tablespoons
light soy sauce .... 1 tablespoon
granulated sugar .... 1 tablespoon
pepper .... pinch
salt

METHOD

Mix the flat strips of steak in a bowl with the soy sauce and cornflour and leave for at least 5 minutes or covered overnight in the refrigerator.

Heat the vegetable oil in a wok or frying pan (skillet) over a high heat, add the steak pieces and flash-fry for a couple of minutes, then lift the steak out of the wok or pan.

To make the sauce, heat the vegetable oil in the same wok or frying pan (don't clean it) as the steak over a high heat, add the onion and a splash of water and fry for a couple of minutes until the onions are slightly softened and lightly browned, then add all the remaining sauce ingredients (except the salt) and let it bubble away for a couple of minutes to reduce.

Add the steak pieces to the sauce, toss through and cook for a further couple of minutes. Taste and season accordingly: it is meant to be tangy, so you may want to add more brown sauce or Worcestershire sauce if necessary.

Serve with steaming hot rice. Sometimes there are some onions and sauce leftover: I am so happy to eat this on its own the next day as it is that tasty!

TOP TIP

Add more vegetables to this dish, such as courgettes (zucchini), mushrooms and sweet (bell) peppers, to make it go even further.

SEAFOOD

The Chinese word for fish is *yu*, which also sounds like the word for 'abundance' (*yoo*) if spoken in Mandarin. A popular symbol during Chinese New Year is a child holding a goldfish. According to Feng Shui, fish and the element water represent prosperity, good fortune and abundance. This is why you find fish and seafood served at big celebration dinners.

When I was growing up in Lisburn, a market town in Northern Ireland, fishmongers and greengrocers had weekly stalls and Mum went every Tuesday without fail: we were very fortunate to be able to try seafood which was not deemed to be part of a typical weekly dinner, such as lobster and turbot.

CHAPTER TWO

SWEET AND SPICY KING PRAWNS	32
CLASSIC HONG KONG-STYLE STEAMED WHOLE FISH	34
DEEP-FRIED FISH CAKES WITH TANGY DIPPING SAUCE	37
GARLICKY SCALLOPS ON GLASS NOODLES	38
GINGER AND SPRING ONION MUSSELS	40
CRISPY FISH WITH SWEETCORN SAUCE	42

Sweet and Spicy King Prawns

In Chinese cuisine, fish and shellfish are greatly enjoyed in their entirety: 'on the bone', with crispy skin, and even shells intact, which all adds extra flavour. This is a lip-smacking dish which Mum used to make after getting fresh king prawns (shrimp) from the Tuesday market. My kids love prawns and will eat them in any form!

Serves: 4
Prep: 5 minutes
Cook: 15 minutes

INGREDIENTS

raw king prawns (shrimp) .... 500 g (1 lb 2 oz)
vegetable oil .... 2 tablespoons
piece of fresh ginger root, sliced ...... 15 g (½ oz)
garlic cloves, crushed 3
dried chilli flakes or oil (or *Suzie's Homemade Chilli Oil*, see page 48) .... 1 teaspoon
tomato ketchup .... 4 tablespoons
sugar .... 2 teaspoons
rice wine vinegar .... 2 tablespoons
Shaoxing wine .... 2 tablespoons
large spring onions (scallions),
    cut into chunks 4

METHOD

Clean the prawns and make a shallow incision down their backs to remove the digestive tract.

Heat the vegetable oil in a wok or large frying pan (skillet) over a high heat. Add the ginger and garlic and fry for a couple of minutes until the aromas are released (be careful they do not burn, adjusting the heat if the mixture starts to catch). Add the chilli flakes or oil and fry for another minute, followed by the ketchup, sugar and vinegar, and let everything bubble away for a couple of minutes, then add the Shaoxing wine and a splash of water. Simmer for a couple of minutes to reduce, then add the prawns and toss so they are evenly coated. Cover the wok or pan with a lid and let the prawns steam for about 5 minutes. Remove the lid and keep stirring until the prawns are cooked through: how long this takes will depend on the size of the prawns.

Finally, mix through the spring onions and serve.

TOP TIP
If you can't get hold of fresh prawns, thawed frozen raw king prawns work really well in this recipe too.

Classic Hong Kong-style Steamed Whole Fish

This dish is simple but absolutely delicious – the flesh is silky smooth from the steaming method and the ginger, spring onion and soy sauce dressing adds a punchy flavour. The Chinese believe you must steam fish whole with the head and tail still intact as it represents family being a whole unit. So, if you cannot fit the fish into the steamer as it is, cut it in half rather than removing the head or tail, which is bad luck.

Serves: 2
Prep: 5 minutes
Cook: 20 minutes

INGREDIENTS

large bunches of spring onions (scallions), white parts sliced lengthways and green ends finely sliced into matchsticks (and put in a bowl of cold water) 2

sea bass, or two smaller white fish, cleaned and gutted (head(s) removed if you wish) .... 500 g/1 lb 2 oz

fresh ginger root, finely sliced into matchsticks .... 15 g (½ oz)

vegetable oil .... 2 tablespoons

light soy sauce .... 4 tablespoons

METHOD

Set up a steamer, half-fill the pan with water and bring to the boil over a high heat.

Put the white parts of the spring onions in a heatproof dish (that will fit in your steamer), place the fish on top and arrange the ginger evenly on top. Place in the steamer and steam for about 12 minutes. After 12 minutes, turn off the heat and leave the lid on for a further 2 minutes.

Heat the vegetable oil in a small saucepan until boiling (test by using the handle end of a wooden spoon – bubbles should fizz around it).

Lift the lid off the heatproof dish, then sprinkle the drained green spring onions on top of the steamed fish and pour over the boiling oil so it lightly 'fries' the spring onions and ginger. Pour the soy sauce over the fish, carefully lift the heatproof dish out of the steamer and serve.

TOP TIPS

If you use a fish other than sea bass, make sure it fits in your steamer, then steam for about 12 minutes for every 500 g (1 lb 2 oz).

The whole fish can also be replaced with the equivalent weight in fish fillets.

Deep-fried Fish Cakes with Tangy Dipping Sauce

We always ordered crispy fish cakes when we went out for dim sum with family in China. I have made these with a high ratio of squid to white fish, so they are quite soft in texture. These fish cakes pair perfectly with the garlicky, sweet and tangy chilli dip.

Makes: 10 fish cakes
Prep: 10 minutes
Cook: 20 minutes

INGREDIENTS

vegetable oil......................................4 tablespoons
cornflour (cornstarch),
    for dusting......................4 heaped tablespoons

DIPPING SAUCE

granulated sugar.............................1 tablespoon
rice wine vinegar.............................1 tablespoon
large fresh chilli, finely chopped.....................1
garlic cloves, finely chopped..........................2

FISH CAKES

squid bodies...............................150 g (5 oz)
white fish fillets such as sea bass, basa or
    pollock, skinless and boneless.....200 g (7 oz)
large garlic clove, finely chopped...................1
salt...½ heaped teaspoon
white pepper...........................½ heaped teaspoon
toasted sesame oil.............................1 teaspoon
cornflour (cornstarch)........1 heaped tablespoon
large spring onion (scallion), thinly sliced.......1

METHOD

Pat the squid and fish dry with paper towel.

To make the dipping sauce, put the sugar, rice wine vinegar and 100 ml (3½ fl oz/scant ½ cup) of water into a small saucepan and bring to the boil. Stir in the chilli and garlic, then remove from the heat and set to one side to infuse.

Cut the squid into small chunks and split between two bowls, putting 100 g (3½ oz) in one bowl and 50 g (1¾ oz) in the other. Put the 100 g (3½ oz) of squid and the fish fillets into the bowl of a food processor with the garlic, salt, pepper, sesame oil and cornflour and blitz until smooth. Add the spring onion and pulse a couple of times. Remove the blade from the bowl and add the 50 g (1¾ oz) of squid chunks (this gives the mixture extra texture) and mix with a wooden spoon.

Heat the vegetable oil in a wok or non-stick frying pan over a high heat and swirl it carefully around so the wok or pan surface is coated in oil. Put the cornflour in a bowl, dip a tablespoon in cold water, then use it to scoop out a large spoonful of the fish and squid mixture and place it in the flour, carefully turning it to coat it on all sides. This forms a barrier and gives the cakes a crispy coating.

Place each fish cake in the hot oil – you can cook a couple at a time – and fry for about a minute on each side until golden. Lift out and place on clean paper towel to drain, then serve with the dipping sauce.

TOP TIP

If you've bought more squid than you need for this recipe, it can be frozen and used again in *Crispy Seafood Noodles* (see page 82).

Garlicky Scallops on Glass Noodles

This may seem like a very luxurious dish, but scallops are actually not that expensive. Luckily, in Northern Ireland, we are blessed with both king (which are bigger in size) and queen scallops all year round. If you can't get your hands on scallops, use giant shelled king prawns (shrimp) instead. There are a number of variations of this steamed scallop dish and it is usually served as part of big Chinese banquets because of seafood's connection to prosperity and fortune.

Serves: 4
Prep: 10 minutes
Cook: 4–8 minutes

INGREDIENTS

dried glass noodles (made with mung
    bean or pea starch) .... 50 g (1¾ oz)
vegetable oil .... 1 tablespoon
XO sauce .... 2 tablespoons
large garlic cloves, finely chopped or grated 2
large fresh scallops (keep the roe intact
    if you wish) 8
clean scallop shells (optional) 8
light soy sauce .... 4 tablespoons
granulated sugar .... 1 level teaspoon
thinly sliced spring onion (scallion) or coriander
    (cilantro), to serve

METHOD

Bring a saucepan of water to the boil, then remove from the heat. Add the dried glass noodles and stir for about 30 seconds. Drain and rinse with cold water in a colander, then set aside. Be careful not to overcook the noodles – you want them to still have a bite.

Clean and dry the pan, then add the oil, XO sauce and garlic, and stir over a high heat for a couple of minutes until sizzling and fragrant. Remove from the heat and set aside.

Set up a steamer, half-fill the pan with water and bring to the boil over a high heat.

If you are using the scallop shells, evenly split the rehydrated glass noodles between the eight shells or place them in a shallow heatproof dish. If you are steaming the scallops in their shells, you may only be able to fit four shells in the steamer at a time, so you will have to steam them in two batches.

Place a scallop on top of each noodle-dressed shell or put them in the dish. Put 1 teaspoon of the XO and garlic oil mixture over the top of each of the eight scallops (do not clean the pan). In the same small pan of XO and garlic mix add the soy sauce, sugar and 50 ml of water and bring to the boil.

Steam the scallops for about 4 minutes (repeat if steaming in batches).

When you take out the scallops, pour some of the soy sauce dressing over the glass noodles under the hot scallops and dress with the spring onions or coriander.

TOP TIP

XO sauce is one of the star ingredients in *XO Sauce Udon Noodles* (see page 128). You can also add a large dollop to the *Instant Noodle Bowl* (see page 118).

Ginger and Spring Onion Mussels

Ginger and spring onion lobster is a well-known celebration dish for Chinese wedding banquets and Lunar New Year meals. Mum made this dish on special occasions or when lobsters were in season, and in the latter years of her life she served it every time my sisters came home from university! I have used mussels here as they are less expensive and more readily available.

Serves: 4
Prep: 20 minutes
Cook: 5–7 minutes

INGREDIENTS

mussels .... 1 kg (2 lb 4 oz)
vegetable oil .... 1 tablespoon
onion, thinly sliced 1
large bunches of spring onions (scallions), white
    parts thinly sliced and green parts cut into
    larger chunks 2
piece of fresh ginger root,
    thinly sliced .... 40 g (1½ oz)
light soy sauce .... 1 tablespoon
oyster sauce .... 2 tablespoons
toasted sesame oil .... ½ tablespoon
white pepper .... ¼ teaspoon
light lager .... 200 ml (7 fl oz/scant 1 cup)

METHOD

Scrub the mussels clean, removing any barnacles from the shells and pulling off the 'beards' with your fingers. Place the mussels in a colander and rinse them thoroughly. Then submerge them in a bowl of cold fresh water for at least 20 minutes, so that the sand inside is cleaned out (the mussels will breathe and 'spit' out the sand). Discard any mussels that remain open when tapped or have cracked shells.

Heat the vegetable oil in a wok or large saucepan over a high heat. Add the onion, white parts of the spring onions and the ginger and fry for a minute or so until the aromas are released. Add the soy sauce, oyster sauce, sesame oil and white pepper and let everything bubble away for a minute or so, then toss in the cleaned mussels and mix well. Add the beer and toss, put the lid on and leave for 3 minutes over a high heat. Lift the lid and check if the shells have all opened. If they haven't, shake the wok or pan with the lid on and cook for a further 1–2 minutes until all the shells have opened. Do not overcook them as they will get very rubbery. If any mussels remain closed after cooking, do not try to open them to eat – discard them immediately. Toss in the green parts of the spring onions and cover until you are ready to serve.

Crispy Fish with Sweetcorn Sauce

This is another childhood favourite which was loved by everyone in my Hong Kong household. This is the perfect dish for the busy mum – one that the kids will eat but which also ticks the boxes in terms of an all-round nutritious and healthy meal. The fish pieces can be prepared ahead and frozen (before frying), saving you time on days when you need dinner on the table super quick.

Serves: 4
Prep: 5 minutes
Cook: 10 minutes

INGREDIENTS

vegetable oil, for frying

FISH PIECES

white fish fillets such as pollock, cod or
    haddock, cut into chunks .... 500 g (1 lb 2 oz)
salt .... ½ teaspoon
white pepper .... ½ teaspoon
large eggs, beaten 2
cornflour
    (cornstarch) .... 100 g (3½ oz/scant 1 cup)
plain (all-purpose) flour ...... 100 g (3½ oz/ ¾ cup)

SWEETCORN SAUCE

tin of creamed corn .... 400g (14 oz)
chicken stock .... 400 ml (13 fl oz/1½ cups)
garlic powder .... 1 teaspoon
salt .... ½ teaspoon
white pepper .... ¼ teaspoon
frozen peas .... 150 g (5 oz)
tinned or fresh sweetcorn .... 150 g (5 oz)
cornflour (cornstarch) paste .... 2 teaspoons
large eggs, beaten 2

METHOD

Preheat the oven to 180°C fan (400°F/gas 6).

Pour vegetable oil into a saucepan to a depth of about 2 cm (¾ in). To test if the oil is ready, check it with the handle of a wooden spoon: the oil should fizz around the spoon immediately.

Season the fish chunks with the salt and pepper. Put the two beaten eggs in a shallow dish and combine the cornflour and flour in a separate shallow dish. Dip the seasoned fish into the beaten egg, then transfer to the flour mixture and toss to coat. Shake the pieces of fish so they don't stick together.

Shallow-fry the coated fish pieces in batches in the hot oil for 5 minutes until golden. Transfer to a grill tray or roasting tin (pan) and place in the oven to keep warm and crispy while you are making the rest of the dish.

To make the sweetcorn sauce, put the creamed corn, chicken stock, garlic powder, salt and pepper, peas and sweetcorn kernels in a wok or saucepan and let everything come to the boil, then boil for 5 minutes. Taste to see whether the sauce needs any more seasoning. Add the cornflour paste and allow it to thicken, then stir the sauce, add the two beaten eggs and keep stirring – this will create the ribbons of cooked egg. Simmer for another 30 seconds or so. Add the crispy fish, toss and serve straight away with a big bowl of steaming hot rice.

MENU PLAN

A Chinese meal is usually made up of at least
two dishes – one meat and one vegetable –
and is always served with big bowls of steaming
hot basmati rice.

◉ STARTERS ◉

CRISPY FISH WITH
SWEETCORN SAUCE

(opposite)

◉ MAIN ◉

CHINESE CABBAGE AND
SHIITAKE MUSHROOMS

(see page 46)

◉ DESSERT ◉

MANGO PUDDING

(see page 164)

VEGGIES

Vegetarian dishes (*so coi*) have always been a key part of Chinese cuisine. My extended family were all brought up in the Buddhist faith. Buddhists do not believe in eating animals and pungent vegetables such as onions and garlic are forbidden In their diet as they are thought to excite one's senses. Buddhist vegetarian dishes were known as *jai choi*. We were not strict Buddhists, but Mum still made meat-free dishes. Nowadays, the concept of meat-free meals is the norm and so are ingredients like tofu. I have modified a few dishes that I love, and created a few new ones as well: I hope you like them.

CHAPTER THREE

CHINESE CABBAGE AND SHIITAKE MUSHROOMS	46
SPICY CRISPY TOFU BITES WITH SUZIE'S CHILLI OIL	48
MIXED VEG STIR-FRY WITH BAMBOO SHOOTS AND WATER CHESTNUTS	51
STUFFED AUBERGINES WITH BLACK BEAN SAUCE	52
GARLIC MIXED MUSHROOMS	54
TOFU PUFF STIR-FRY	56

Chinese Cabbage and Shiitake Mushrooms

Chinese cabbage (*choi sum*) is quick and easy to cook and is available all year round. This dish is super versatile – opt for whatever greens you have to hand: I like to add the Chinese vegetable *kai lan* (Chinese broccoli). I love the texture it brings to a dish, just so long as it is not overcooked! You can either steam or stir-fry the vegetables; I cut them into similar-sized chunks so they cook evenly.

Serves: 2 as main or 4 as a side
Prep: 5 minutes, plus 10 minutes' soaking time
Cook: 15 minutes

INGREDIENTS

dried shiitake mushrooms .... 60 g (2¼ oz)
    or fresh shiitake or brown
    chestnut mushrooms .... 300 g (10½ oz)
vegetable oil .... 1 tablespoon
large garlic clove, thinly sliced 1
piece of fresh ginger root,
    thinly sliced .... 10 g (¼ oz)
choi sum, *kai lan*, tenderstem broccoli, spring
    greens, green beans, kale or chard, cut into
    4–5 cm (1.5–2 in) pieces .... 200 g (7 oz)
mushroom soaking liquid or
    vegetable stock ... 200 ml (7 fl oz/scant 1 cup)
light soy sauce .... 1 teaspoon
oyster sauce .... 1 teaspoon
cornflour (cornstarch) paste
    (optional) .... 2 teaspoons
sea salt and freshly ground black pepper

METHOD

If you're using dried shiitake mushrooms, put them in a heatproof bowl and pour over enough boiling water to cover them (at least 200 ml/ 7 fl oz/scant 1 cup). Place a small bowl or sieve on top to make sure that all the mushrooms are submerged in the water and leave them to rehydrate for at least 10 minutes. Drain and reserve the soaking liquid.

Thickly slice the drained and rehydrated (or fresh) mushrooms.

Heat the vegetable oil in a wok or large frying pan (skillet) over a high heat, then add the garlic and ginger and fry for a couple of minutes until fragrant, being careful not to burn them. Add the green vegetables and toss them through the fragrant oil, then add the sliced mushrooms with the mushroom liquid (or vegetable stock if you are using fresh mushrooms), light soy sauce and oyster sauce. Cover and steam for 5 minutes over a high heat until the vegetables are just tender. Taste and adjust the seasoning according to preference.

If you want a thicker sauce, add the cornflour paste and bring the mixture to the boil and the sauce will thicken.

Spicy Crispy Tofu Bites with Suzie's Chilli Oil

I am very fond of tofu and I created this dish after making a batch of my sesame peanut bars when I had lots of sesame seeds leftover. My chilli oil is so quick to make and helps add a kick to so many dishes. You will only need a couple of tablespoons for this dish, but this recipe will make more than enough for all the recipes in this book!

Serves: 4
Prep: 15 minutes
Cook: 30 minutes

INGREDIENTS

extra-firm tofu, cut into bite-sized cubes and
    drained well on paper towel .... 400 g (14 oz)
white sesame seeds,
    plus extra for sprinkling .... 80 g (3 oz)
vegetable oil, for frying
spring onions (scallions), sliced, to garnish

MARINADE

toasted sesame oil .... 1 teaspoon
dark soy sauce .... 1 teaspoon
salt .... ¼ teaspoon
white pepper .... ½ teaspoon
small egg 1
cornflour (cornstarch) .... 1 teaspoon

SAUCE

Suzie's Chilli Oil (see below) .... 2 tablespoons
hoisin sauce .... 4 tablespoons
garlic cloves, finely chopped or grated 2
granulated sugar .... 2 teaspoons
dried chilli flakes, to taste (optional)

SUZIE'S CHILLI OIL (MAKES 1 LARGE JAR, OR 2 OR 3 SMALLER JARS)

groundnut oil
    or vegetable oil .... 250 ml (8½ fl oz/1 cup)
sesame seeds .... 4 tablespoons
dried chilli flakes .... 1 heaped tablespoon
chilli powder .... 1 teaspoon
Chinese five-spice powder .... ½ teaspoon
sesame oil .... ½ teaspoon
garlic cloves, finely chopped or grated 2
white pepper .... ½ teaspoon
salt .... ½ teaspoon
dark soy sauce .... 3 tablespoons

METHOD

Whisk all the ingredients for the marinade together in a bowl with a fork. Add the cubed tofu, toss to coat and leave it to sit for at least 5 minutes or, if preparing in advance, leave covered overnight in the refrigerator.

When you're ready to cook the tofu, put the sesame seeds on a lipped plate. Heat about 4 tablespoons of vegetable oil in a wok or frying pan (skillet) over a high heat, then carefully take each piece of marinated tofu and dip it into the sesame seeds (cover all sides). Fry the tofu in batches. Remove each batch with tongs and drain on paper towel.

When all the tofu is cooked, wipe the wok or frying pan clean with paper towel, then add the sauce ingredients and a splash of water and let it bubble away for 3–5 minutes until sticky and thick. Toss in the tofu and cook for a few more minutes, then garnish with the spring onions, sprinkle with extra sesame seeds, and serve.

SUZIE'S CHILLI OIL METHOD

Bring the groundnut or vegetable oil to the boil in a saucepan. To check if it's ready, test it with the handle of a wooden spoon: the oil should fizz around the spoon immediately. Turn off the heat. Leave the oil to sit for a couple of minutes.

While the oil cools, toss the sesame seeds in a dry frying pan (skillet) over a high heat for a couple of minutes until they turn slightly golden. Place the toasted sesame seeds, dried chilli flakes, chilli powder, Chinese five-spice powder, sesame oil, garlic, pepper and salt in a large, clean jar, then carefully pour over the hot oil.

Once the oil is fully cooled, add the soy sauce and mix. It is now ready to use and will keep in the fridge for up to 1 month.

MENU PLAN

There is no perfect combination of dishes for a Chinese meal – it really is all up to you and what you have to hand. However, this is a simple vegetarian-focused menu plan that can be achieved with little effort.

❀ STARTERS ❀

MIXED VEG STIR-FRY WITH BAMBOO SHOOTS AND WATER CHESTNUTS

(opposite)

❀ MAIN ❀

GARLIC MIXED MUSHROOMS

(see page 54)

❀ DESSERT ❀

HONG KONG-STYLE FRENCH TOAST

(see page 150)

Mixed Veg Stir-fry with Bamboo Shoots and Water Chestnuts

Bamboo shoots come in lots of different varieties and need to be cooked before they can be eaten. Water chestnuts, however, can be eaten raw or cooked. Both have been used in Chinese cuisine for centuries and I think they are very underrated as vegetables. I always have a couple of tins of each in my cupboard as they are great for bulking out dishes and quick stir-fries, such as this.

Serves: 4
Prep: 5 minutes
Cook: 15 minutes

INGREDIENTS

vegetable oil .... 2 tablespoons
piece of fresh ginger root,
    finely sliced .... 10 g (¼ oz)
garlic cloves, finely sliced 2
red chilli, thinly sliced 1
onion, thinly sliced 1
large carrot, peeled and thinly sliced
    into rounds 1
mangetout (snow peas),
    sliced diagonally .... 250 g (9 oz)
baby sweetcorn, sliced diagonally .... 250 g (9 oz)
tin of bamboo shoots, drained .... 225 g (8 oz)
tin of water chestnuts, drained .... 225 g (8 oz)
oyster sauce or vegetarian
    stir-fry sauce .... 4 tablespoons
Shaoxing wine .... 1 tablespoon
toasted sesame oil .... 1 teaspoon
vegetable stock (optional) .... 100–200 ml
    (3½–7fl oz/scant ½ cup–scant 1 cup)
cornflour (cornstarch) paste
    (optional) .... 2 teaspoons
sea salt and freshly ground black pepper

METHOD

Heat the vegetable oil in a wok or frying pan (skillet) over a high heat, then add the ginger, garlic and chilli and fry for about a minute, being careful not to burn the vegetables – they will smell aromatic. Add the onion, carrot, mangetout, baby sweetcorn, bamboo shoots and water chestnuts and toss, then add the oyster sauce (or vegetarian equivalent), Shaoxing wine and sesame oil and let everything bubble away for about 5 minutes. Taste and adjust for seasoning. If you want more sauce, add 100–200 ml (3½–7 fl oz/scant ½ cup–scant 1 cup) of vegetable stock.

If you prefer a thicker sauce, add the cornflour paste and bring to the boil and it will thicken up.

Enjoy the stir-fry with rice or noodles, or on its own.

TOP TIP

Use any vegetables you have to hand for this dish – carrots, onions, courgettes (zucchini), sweet (bell) peppers, mushrooms ... the options are endless!

Stuffed Aubergines with Black Bean Sauce

Mum's version of this dish was originally made with minced (ground) pork and king prawns (shrimp); she used to stuff peppers, aubergines (eggplant) and tofu with this mixture. She would pan-fry these to sear them and then pop them into a steamer until they were cooked all the way through before topping with a rich black bean sauce. I adapted this recipe because I always have a meat-free mince alternative in the freezer.

Serves: 4
Prep: 15 minutes
Cook: 25 minutes

INGREDIENTS

medium aubergine (eggplant) 1
cornflour (cornstarch),
    for dusting .... 4 tablespoons
vegetable oil, for frying
spring onions (scallions), thinly sliced, to garnish

STUFFING

quorn mince .... 100 g (3½ oz)
mushrooms, finely chopped .... 50 g (1¾ oz)
spring onion (scallion), thinly sliced 1
1 small egg 1
cornflour (cornstarch) .... 1 heaped teaspoon
light soy sauce .... 1 tablespoon
toasted sesame oil .... 1 teaspoon
sea salt and freshly ground white pepper .... pinch

BLACK BEAN SAUCE

vegetable oil
garlic, finely chopped
    or grated .... 1 heaped teaspoon
finely chopped fresh ginger root .... 1 teaspoon
dried fermented black beans, soaked
    in water then drained .... 1 tablespoon
light soy sauce .... 2 teaspoons
vegetable stock powder .... 1 teaspoon
cornflour (cornstarch) paste .... 2 teaspoons

TOP TIP

To make the fermented black beans, put them in a small bowl and cover with boiling water. Let stand for 15 minutes, then pour off the excess water just before using.

METHOD

Chop off the top of the aubergine, then halve it lengthways and place the halves, cut side down, on a chopping board. Cut 1.5-cm (⅝-in) wide chunks – these will resemble semi-circles if you look at them side on. Then carefully make a big slit down the middle, from the rounded skin side to 3–4mm (⅛–¼ in) from the bottom flat white edge of the aubergine (be careful not to slice all the way through).

Mix the stuffing ingredients in a bowl until everything is well combined. Using a teaspoon, take some of the stuffing mixture and put it into the middle of the sliced aubergine. Repeat until all the mixture or aubergine is used up, then dust the aubergine sides lightly with cornflour.

Prepare a steamer or pan (with a trivet) for steaming and bring the water to the boil.

Heat 3 tablespoons of vegetable oil in a wok or frying pan (skillet) over a high heat, add the aubergine and fry until lightly brown. You may have to do this in batches. Transfer the aubergine to a heatproof dish that will fit in the steamer or pan. Place the dish in the steamer or pan and steam for about 10 minutes, until the aubergine is soft. Remove from the heat.

To make the sauce, heat a splash of oil in a saucepan over a high heat, add the garlic and ginger and fry for about 30 seconds, then add the drained black beans, soy sauce, stock powder and 200 ml (7 fl oz/scant 1 cup) water. Let this bubble away for 5 minutes, taste and season accordingly. To thicken, add the cornflour paste and bring to the boil.

Pour the sauce over the stuffed aubergine and garnish with spring onions.

Garlic Mixed Mushrooms

I love mushrooms and this recipe pays homage to the humble yet delicious fungi. I have used a variety of mushrooms, from dried to fresh, and I am also introducing you to lily flowers or buds, which are available in Asian supermarkets or online. They add an earthy flavour and amazing texture. This dish is not limited to mushrooms, however. Garlic goes with anything, really, so add other vegetables as you wish!

Serves: 4
Prep: 10 minutes, plus minimum 15 minutes' soaking time
Cook: 25 minutes

INGREDIENTS

dried black fungus	15 g (½ oz)
dried lily flowers or buds	15 g (½ oz)
vegetable oil	2 tablespoons
large garlic cloves, thinly sliced	3
oyster sauce or vegetarian stir-fry sauce	4 tablespoons
Shaoxing wine	1 tablespoon
white mushrooms, halved or quartered	50 g (1¾ oz)
chestnut mushrooms, halved or quartered	50 g (1¾ oz)
tin of whole straw mushrooms in water	425 g (15 oz)
pak choi, halved lengthways	125 g (4½ oz)
sea salt and freshly ground black pepper	
cornflour (cornstarch) paste	2 teaspoons

METHOD

Rehydrate the dried black fungus and lily flowers or buds in boiling water in seperate bowls for at least 15 minutes. (They can be left to soak for up to 1 hour.)

Heat the vegetable oil in a wok or frying pan (skillet) over a high heat, add the garlic and fry for 2–3 minutes until fragrant, then add the oyster sauce (or vegetarian equivalent) and Shaoxing wine and cook for a few more minutes. Add the black fungus, lily flowers or buds, white mushrooms, chestnut mushrooms and straw mushrooms with the water from the tin, then add in about 250 ml (8½ fl oz/ 1 cup) of the rehydrated black fungus and lily flower/ bud liquid.

Simmer for 10 minutes, so that the flavours infuse, then add the pak choi and cook for a further 5 minutes. Taste and season. If you would like more sauce, add more of the rehydrating liquid and taste and season as needed. To thicken the sauce, add the cornflour paste and bring to the boil, then let it bubble away for a few minutes before taking off the heat.

This is delicious with a big bowl of rice or tossed through noodles.

TOP TIP

Black fungus and lily flowers are also used in the *Hot and Sour Soup* on page 137 and can be added to other stir-fry dishes.

Tofu Puff Stir-fry

Tofu puffs are such a versatile ingredient and are a great addition to stir-fries, soups, stews and curries. They are like sponges, soaking up the flavour of the dish and tantalising your taste buds with every bite.

Serves: 4
Prep: 30 minutes, including 20 minutes' soaking time
Cook: 20 minutes

INGREDIENTS

dried shiitake mushrooms .... 40 g (1½ oz)
vegetable oil .... 1 tablespoon
garlic cloves, thinly sliced 2
piece of fresh ginger root,
   thinly sliced .... 10 g (¼ oz)
oyster sauce or vegetarian
   stir-fry sauce .... 3 generous tablespoons
light soy sauce .... 2 teaspoons
toasted sesame oil .... 1 teaspoon
tofu puffs .... 250 g (9 oz)
medium carrot, peeled and
   thinly sliced on the diagonal 1
seasonal green vegetables
   (optional) .... about 100 g (3½ oz)
sea salt and freshly ground black pepper
spring onions (scallions), sliced diagonally,
   to garnish 2

METHOD

Soak the dried shiitake mushrooms in 500 ml (17 fl oz/2 cups) of just-boiled water for at least 15 minutes – do this in a heatproof jug to make it easier to see how much water you have added. The mushrooms can soak for 1 hour. Strain and keep the mushroom soaking liquid for the sauce.

Heat the vegetable oil in a wok or frying pan (skillet) over a high heat, add the garlic and ginger and fry for a couple of minutes. Add the oyster sauce (or vegetarian equivalent), light soy sauce, sesame oil and the mushroom soaking liquid, then add the tofu puffs and simmer for 10 minutes.

Add the drained shiitake mushrooms, the carrot and seasonal greens (if using) and simmer for another 10 minutes, pushing the tofu puffs down with a wooden spoon so they are submerged in the cooking liquid. You want to make sure the flavours have penetrated the middle of each tofu puff.

Taste and adjust the seasoning according to preference, then plate up and sprinkle with the spring onions.

TOP TIP

The tofu puffs can be used as a substitute for the beef in the *Beef and Black Bean Sauce* recipe (page 144) for a delicious veggie option.

DIM SUM AND DUMPLINGS

I was lucky enough to be able to eat my way around Hong Kong when I was young. I loved going for breakfast, especially for dim sum (*yum cha*), which is an ancient Chinese tradition of drinking tea while eating small bite-sized dishes. The variety of dim sum can range from braised chicken feet to pork (*siu mai*) and shrimp (*haa gaau*).

Not only is dim sum one of the most famous foods to eat in Hong Kong, but eating it is one of the most fun and delicious food experiences you can have.

My little ones now ask for dim sum dumplings every week, so I have developed a few recipes that enable me to make them using ingredients from my local shop.

CHAPTER FOUR

PRAWN DUMPLINGS	61
PORK AND PRAWN DUMPLINGS	62
CHICKEN CONGEE WITH DEEP-FRIED SAVOURY DONUT STICKS	67
TURKEY POT STICKERS	68
SAUSAGE MEAT AND SPRING ONION DUMPLINGS	70
STICKY PORK BELLY BAO BUNS WITH SUZIE'S PICKLED VEGETABLES	72

Prawn Dumplings

Dim sum is not really dim sum without prawns (*haa gaau*) or pork (*siu mai*). These prawn dumplings are encased in a crystal-smooth wrapper and are deemed one of the classics of dim sum. There should be at least seven pleats in the outer casing and this should be thin and translucent but sturdy enough not to break when picked up, so you can eat them in one bite. This family-friendly recipe will start you on your journey to making dumplings from scratch.

Makes: 16 dumplings
Prep: 25 minutes
Cook: 12–16 minutes

INGREDIENTS

thin slices of peeled carrot, for the
    haa gaau (optional) 16
wonton wrappers (or see the
    Wrapper Dough recipe on page 10) 16

PRAWN FILLING

king prawns (shrimp),
    peeled and coarsely chopped ...... 75 g (2½ oz)
king prawns (shrimp),
    peeled and finely chopped .... 175 g (6 oz)
toasted sesame oil .... 1 teaspoon
vegetable oil .... 1 tablespoon
grated fresh ginger root .... 1 heaped teaspoon
bamboo shoots, finely chopped ...... 50 g (1¾ oz)
salt .... ¼ teaspoon
white pepper .... ¼ teaspoon
granulated sugar .... ½ teaspoon
oyster sauce .... 2 teaspoons
cornflour (cornstarch) .... 1 heaped teaspoon

METHOD

Put all the prawn filling ingredients in a bowl and mix until well combined. Cover and place in the fridge until needed.

If making the wrapper dough from scratch, follow the instructions on page 10.

Set up a steamer, half-fill the pan with water and bring to the boil over a high heat. Leave off the top steamer section (the bit with holes) so you can fit the *haa gaau* inside when they are ready to be steamed.

Place a wrapper in the palm of your hand and put a teaspoon of mixture in the middle, then hold with both hands. Fold up one side and then make one pleat in the dough on the opposite side nearest the fold, using your fingers and thumbs, and pinch it closed. Repeat the pleating as many times as you can until the whole prawn filling is enclosed. If there is excess dough on top of the dumpling, trim it off with scissors. It should look round at the bottom and pleated on top: see image on page 64. Repeat with the remaining wrappers and filling. Place each dumpling on a slice of carrot (if using) or line the perforated section of the steamer with a disc of baking parchment pierced with holes and place in the top part of the steamer, spreading them out evenly (you'll probably need to steam them in batches). Cover and steam for 6–8 minutes until cooked through, glistening and transparent. Serve straight away. These are delicious with my chilli sauce (see page 48), with soy sauce or on their own!

Pork and Prawn Dumplings

Pork (*siu mai*) is another dim sum classic ordered with prawn (shrimp) dim sum (*haa gaau*). The wonton wrapper, shaped like a tiny cup, is stuffed with pork, prawn and mushrooms and steamed perfectly to give you a delightful taste explosion in just one mouthful. Traditionally *siu mai* is topped with fish roe, but for this recipe, I have used grated carrot instead.

Makes: 24 dumplings
Prep: 10 minutes
Cook: 10-20 minutes

INGREDIENTS

wonton wrappers (from your local Asian supermarket)	24
carrot, peeled and grated	1

PORK AND PRAWN FILLING

light soy sauce	2 teaspoons
king prawns, finely chopped	125 g (4½ oz)
minced (ground) pork (at least 15% fat)	250 g (9 oz)
shiitake mushrooms, finely diced (use 10 g/ ½ oz) or dried shiitake mushrooms soaked according to the packet instructions if you can't find fresh)	30 g (1 oz)
finely diced white part of spring onions (scallions)	2 heaped teaspoons
finely grated fresh ginger root or ground ginger	1 teaspoon
salt	½ teaspoon
sugar	¼ teaspoon
pepper	pinch
Shaoxing wine	2 teaspoons
toasted sesame oil	1 teaspoon
oyster sauce	2 teaspoons
cornflour (cornstarch)	1½ teaspoons

METHOD

Put all the pork and prawn filling ingredients in a bowl and mix until well combined. (If you wish, you can roughly chop the prawns, mushrooms and spring onions and then pulse everything in a food processor until combined.) Cover and place in the fridge until needed.

Set up a steamer, half-fill the pan with water and bring to the boil over a high heat. Leave off the top steamer section (the bit with holes).

With one hand turned so your thumb and index finger are horizontal, touch the thumb and index together, then gently ease a wonton wrapper into the circular gap you have created so it acts like a tiny net. Using a teaspoon, pack with filling until it reaches the top. Some pointed ends of the wrapper will stick out – you can leave these or stick them to the side of the *siu mai* with a little water. Add a pinch of grated carrot on top of each one.

Line the perforated section of the steamer with a disc of baking parchment pierced with holes and place the *siu mai* in the top part of the steamer, spreading them out evenly (you'll probably need to steam them in batches). Cover and steam for 8–10 minutes until cooked through. Eat immediately.

TOP TIP

These delicious dumplings can be frozen (you will need to add about 5 minutes' extra steaming time if cooking from frozen) so make a double batch and pop them in the freezer to enjoy whenever you have a craving.

Prawn
Dumplings 61

Pork and Prawn
Dumplings 62

Chicken Congee with Deep-fried Savoury Donut Sticks

Families often add lots more water to a pot of rice to stretch it out, making rice porridge or congee. Mum used to make this for us when we were being weaned and also, as in many Chinese families, when we were ill. It is such a comforting recipe. Congee can be plain as you like but the toppings and flavours are endless! Savoury donuts are always served with congee (well, in my experience, anyway).

Makes: 10 donuts
Serves: 4
Prep: 20 minutes, plus 1 hour proving
Cook: 45 minutes

INGREDIENTS

CHICKEN CONGEE

chicken breast, skinless and
    thinly sliced .... 250 g (9 oz)
cornflour (cornstarch) .... 1 teaspoon
light soy sauce .... 1 teaspoon
oyster sauce .... 1 teaspoon
basmati rice .... 100 g (3½ oz/½ cup)
chicken stock powder .... ½ teaspoon
piece of fresh ginger root,
    thinly sliced .... 10 g (¼ oz)
sea salt and white pepper

DEEP-FRIED SAVOURY DONUT STICKS

large egg 1
self-raising flour, plus extra
    for rolling .... 200 g (7 oz/1⅔ cup)
bicarbonate of soda (baking soda) .... ⅛ teaspoon
salt .... ¼ teaspoon
vegetable oil, plus extra
    for greasing .... 1 tablespoon

GARNISH

piece of fresh ginger root,
    thinly sliced .... 40 g (1½ oz)
spring onions (scallions), thinly sliced 2

METHOD

Put the chicken in a bowl with the cornflour, soy sauce and oyster sauce. Cover and leave for at least 1 hour 15 minutes or overnight in the refrigerator.

To make the dough for the donut sticks, follow the instructions on page 10.

Rinse the rice three times in cold water in a bowl (replenishing the water each time you rinse), then bring 1 litre (34 fl oz/4 cups) of water to the boil. Stir in the chicken stock powder, then add the washed rice and stir. Bring back to the boil, then reduce the heat, put a lid on (slightly ajar) and simmer for 25–30 minutes, giving it an occasional stir. Once cooked, mix rapidly with a wooden spoon or whisk and check that the rice grains are fluffy. Once the rice base is ready, add the marinated chicken a little at a time so that the pieces don't clump together, stirring continuously. Add the ginger and cook for another couple of minutes until the chicken is cooked. Taste and season accordingly.

Heat 3–4 cm (1¼–1½ in) of vegetable oil in a wok or saucepan over a high heat for frying the donuts. Test if the oil is ready for frying with the handle of a wooden spoon: the oil should fizz around the spoon immediately.

Lift each end of a piece of donut dough carefully with both hands and stretch it out just a little so it is still even in width, then gently lower it into the hot oil and fry for a couple of minutes on each side until golden, using tongs or chopsticks to help turn the donut. Drain on paper towel and repeat for the remaining donuts.

Serve with a garnish of ginger and spring onion and the savoury donut sticks on the side.

Turkey Pot Stickers

These dumplings have so many different names – I know them in Cantonese as *wo tip*. Pot stickers is the name given to them due to the method in which they are cooked. Traditional dumplings are made with different fillings, such as meat and vegetables, and encased in a homemade wrapper. Each region in China has their own take on this dumpling, so the variety is endless. Pork is one of the most popular ingredients to use, but I decided to play around with turkey mince to make them leaner.

Makes: 40 pot stickers
Prep: 15 minutes, plus 1 hour resting time
Cook: 30 minutes

INGREDIENTS

gyoza wrappers (or see the *Gyoza Wrapper* recipe on page 10) 40

DIPPING SAUCE

rice vinegar (or any vinegar) .... 2 tablespoons
light soy sauce .... 2 tablespoons
chilli, thinly sliced .... ½
toasted sesame oil .... 1 teaspoon

FILLING

sesame oil .... 1 teaspoon
mushrooms, finely chopped .... about 100 g (3½ oz)
salt .... ½ teaspoon
quorn or turkey mince (broken down even further into finer mince lumps) .... 200 g (7 oz)
spring onions (scallions), thinly sliced 2
large garlic cloves, grated or crushed 2
piece of fresh ginger root, grated ...... 15 g (½ oz)
sesame oil .... 2 teaspoons
small egg, beaten 1
cornflour (cornstarch) .... 2 teaspoons
dark soy sauce .... 2 teaspoons
pepper .... ½ teaspoon
chilli, finely chopped (optional) .... ½

FOR FRYING

vegetable oil .... 1 teaspoon
toasted sesame oil .... 2 teaspoons

METHOD

If making the wrapper dough from scratch, follow the instructions on page 10.

Mix all the sauce ingredients together in a bowl. Cover and keep in the fridge until needed.

To make the filling, heat the sesame oil in a frying pan (skillet) over a high heat. Add the mushrooms and salt and fry for a few minutes until the mushrooms have shrunk. Mix the mince with the remaining filling ingredients in a bowl.

Place a wrapper in the palm of your hand and put a heaped teaspoon of filling in the middle. Dip a finger in a bowl of water and dampen the edge of the wrapper all the way around. Fold the wrapper in half over the filling and pinch the centre with your fingers. Remember, your dumpling should have a flat part (the back piece of pastry) and a pleated part (the front). Using your thumb and index finger, pleat the pastry towards the middle of the dumpling on one side and then switch to the other side, you will get about three or four pleats on each side. Press the pleats tightly against the back part of the wrapper using your thumb and index finger. Repeat until all the filling is used up.

Heat the vegetable oil in a frying pan over a medium heat, then arrange the *wo tip,* flat side down, in the pan. Fry for a couple of minutes until they turn slightly brown, then add 125 ml (4¼ fl oz/generous ½ cup) of water, cover with a lid and steam for about 5 minutes. Once the water has nearly all evaporated, remove the lid, add 1 teaspoon of sesame oil, then cook for 3 minutes until the bottoms of the dumplings are crispy. Repeat until all are cooked!

Sausage Meat and Spring Onion Dumplings

Baozi is a steamed or fried dumpling with a fluffy casing that can be stuffed with an endless variety of fillings. My favourite type of *baozi* is the *char siu* or chicken bao, which is a Hong Kong delicacy, although the dough takes six days to make as it begins with a sourdough starter (so I'll show you that one another day!). My children can't get enough dumplings of any sort, so I developed this recipe when they begged for them and I literally had nothing else in my house for a filling except a packet of sausages and some spring onions (scallions)!

Makes: 12 dumplings
Prep: 20 minutes, plus 30 minutes' proving time
Cook: 10–20 minutes

INGREDIENTS

BAOZI DOUGH

granulated sugar	8 g (¼ oz)
sachet of fast-action dried yeast	7 g (¼ oz)
plain (all-purpose) flour, plus extra for dusting	200 g (7 oz/1⅔ cup)
baking powder	½ teaspoon
vegetable oil, plus extra for greasing	1 teaspoon

FILLING

pork sausage meat	300 g (10½ oz)
spring onions (scallions), finely chopped	40 g (1½ oz)
toasted sesame oil	1 teaspoon
ground ginger	1 teaspoon
garlic powder granules	½ teaspoon
light soy sauce	1 tablespoon
ground white pepper	½ teaspoon

METHOD

Combine the ingredients for the filling in a bowl, mix well, cover and keep in the fridge until needed. The filling can be made the day before.

To make the *baozi* dough, follow the instructions on page 11.

Put 1 teaspoon (about 30 g/1 oz) of filling in the middle of a circle of dough, then pull any edge up and create a pleat by folding the edge of the dough back on itself using your thumb and index finger to crimp it. Repeat this crimping action, turning the *baozi* in your hand until the whole top is pleated and crimped and you're back to the start: there will be a small hole at the top of the *baozi*, which will allow the steam to escape.

Set up a steamer, half-fill the pan with water and bring to the boil over a high heat. Line the perforated section of the steamer with a disc of baking parchment pierced with holes and place the *baozi* in the steamer. Steam for 12 minutes until cooked, then eat immediately.

If you want the *baozi* to have a crispy base and fluffy interior, pan-fry them on one or both sides before steaming: heat a tablespoon of oil in a frying pan (skillet) over a medium to high heat, add the *baozi* and fry for about 5 minutes, hole-side facing up, being careful not to burn the bottom of the *baozi*. Add just enough water to cover the surface of the pan, then cover and steam for about 5 minutes.

TOP TIPS

Using sausages is a great alternative to minced (ground) pork as they are already seasoned. You can use chicken sausages to make the *baozis* a little healthier, if you wish.

This is an easy recipe to get little ones involved in, mixing, rolling and assembling the *baozi*!

Sticky Pork Belly Bao Buns with Suzie's Pickled Vegetables

Bao buns have been popping up on menus all over the world. I have grown up knowing and eating them. In Hong Kong, they are known as *cha bao* as they are usually pierced with a fork or toothpick to keep the fillings in. You can now buy bao buns in the supermarket, but making them from scratch is quite easy and very satisfying.

Makes: 16 bao buns
Prep: 40 minutes, plus 30 minutes proving time
Cook: 45 minutes–1 hour

INGREDIENTS

bao buns (or see the *Bao Buns* recipes
on page 11) 16

PORK BELLY
slow-roast pork belly,
cut into bite-sized pieces .... 600 g (1 lb 5 oz)

GLAZE
light soy sauce .... 2 tablespoons
piece of fresh ginger root, grated ...... 20 g (¾ oz)
large garlic clove, grated 1
honey .... 1 tablespoon
light brown sugar .... 1 tablespoon
rice wine vinegar .... 2 teaspoons
red chilli, finely chopped (optional) 1

PICKLED VEGETABLES
cucumber, cut lengthways into 5 cm (2 in)
julienne, seeds scraped out
using a teaspoon 1
sea salt .... 2 teaspoons
granulated sugar .... 200 g (7 oz)
rice wine vinegar .... 200 ml (7 fl oz/scant 1 cup)
piece of fresh root ginger,
thinly sliced .... 30 g (1 oz)
medium carrots, peeled and cut lengthways
into 5 cm (2 in) matchsticks 3
white cabbage, thinly shredded .... ¼

TO SERVE
spring onions (scallions), to garnish
green (bell) pepper, cut into thin strips 1
salad leaves .... 2 large handfuls

METHOD

To prepare the pickled vegetables put the cucumber in a sieve or colander and sprinkle over 1 teaspoon of the salt. Leave for at least 10–15 minutes. Pat the cucumber dry with thick paper towel.

Put a saucepan on a set of scales and add 100 g (3½ oz) water, the sugar, rice wine vinegar, the remaining teaspoon of salt and the sliced ginger and bring to the boil for 5 minutes until the sugar has dissolved. Place the vegetables in a clean heatproof jar and pour the pickling liquid over the veg, making sure they are submerged. Leave to cool before sealing.

If making the bao buns from scratch, follow the instructions on page 11.

Set up a steamer, half-fill the pan with water and bring to the boil over a high heat. Line the perforated section of the steamer with a disc of baking parchment pierced with holes.

Place four buns on a heatproof dish in the steamer on top of baking parchment, then put another sheet of parchment on top. Steam over a high heat for 12–15 minutes.

While the buns are steaming, make the glaze. Place all the ingredients in a pan and simmer gently for about 5 minutes, then toss in the pork pieces and coat.

To serve, open the bao sandwich and fill with the pork, some pickled veg and spring onions, peppers and salad leaves. Repeat!

RICE AND NOODLES

Carbs are a must in our household and I cook endless rice and noodle dishes. I could fill a whole book with these recipes, but here are six of my top-rated simplest dishes to get you started.

CHAPTER FIVE

YIN YANG FRIED RICE	76
HOMEMADE WONTON SOUP NOODLES	78
CHEUNG FUN NOODLE BOWL	81
CRISPY SEAFOOD NOODLES	82
VEGGIE SINGAPORE NOODLES	84
DUCK AND PINEAPPLE FRIED RICE	86

Yin Yang Fried Rice

This is a celebratory Hong Kong dish which is served at banquets and weddings. It is called 'yin yang' because it brings together two unlikely pairings: a red dish of tomatoes, chicken and onions and a white dish of prawns and egg whites with peas, served to resemble the symbol of the black and white, interlocking teardrops.

Serves: 6
Prep: 10 minutes
Cook: 25 minutes

INGREDIENTS

large eggs 4
vegetable oil .... 2 tablespoons
cooked basmati rice .... 600 g (1 lb 5 oz)
   (about 200 g/7 oz/1 cup dried rice)
light soy sauce .... 2 tablespoons
sea salt and freshly ground black pepper

RED SAUCE

vegetable oil .... 1 tablespoon
small onion, thinly sliced 1
cooked chicken breast,
   thinly sliced .... 1 (about 200 g/7 oz)
medium tomatoes, thinly sliced 2
tomato ketchup .... 5 tablespoons
granulated sugar .... 1 teaspoon
chicken stock .... about 250 ml (8½ fl oz/1 cup)
cornflour (cornstarch) paste .... 2 teaspoons

WHITE SAUCE

chicken stock .... about 500 ml (17 fl oz/2 cups)
peas .... 70 g (2½ oz)
cornflour (cornstarch) paste .... 2 teaspoons
toasted sesame oil .... 1 teaspoon
king prawns, digestive tract removed and
   butterflied .... 150 g (5 oz)

METHOD

Separate the eggs, putting the yolks and whites into two separate bowls. Beat the egg yolks.

To fry the rice, heat 1 tablespoon of the oil in a wok or frying pan (skillet) over a high heat, add the beaten egg yolks and cook for about 1 minute – you want them to set and form an omelette. Transfer to a plate. Heat the second tablespoon of oil in the wok or frying pan, add the cooked rice and use a wooden spoon to break up the clumps. Add the soy sauce and a large pinch each of salt and pepper. Stir, add the cooked egg yolks and break them up through the rice, cooking for about 5 minutes.

Put the fried rice in a large shallow dish, cover with foil to keep warm and set aside.

To make the red sauce, clean the wok or frying pan. Return it to a high heat with the oil, add the onion with a splash of water and fry for about 1 minute. Add the chicken and cook for a further minute, then add the tomatoes, ketchup and sugar and let everything bubble away for another minute. Stir in the stock, then taste and adjust the seasoning as required. Add the cornflour paste and bring to the boil to thicken. If the sauce is too thick, just add a little more stock. Pour this onto one side of the fried rice.

To make the white sauce, clean the wok or frying pan again, pour in the stock, add the peas and cornflour paste, bring to the boil and allow to thicken. Stir with a wooden spoon, then pour in the egg whites you set aside earlier and swirl to form flecks of cooked white through the sauce. Add the sesame oil and prawns and cook for a couple of minutes until the prawns are cooked through. Taste and season accordingly. Pour the prawn and pea sauce over the other side of the fried rice and serve straight away.

Homemade Wonton Soup Noodles

Wontons are such a great addition to a noodle soup and they can turn a side dish into a main meal. The key to any homemade egg noodle is the *kai sun*, an alkaline substance that changes the gluten structure of the flour, giving the noodles that characteristic bite. *Kai sun* is the baked bicarbonate of soda (baking soda) and is super easy to make. However, you can also buy the liquid form, which is called Lye water, in a bottle.

Serves: 4
Prep: 15 minutes
Cook: 40 minutes

INGREDIENTS

fine dried egg noodles (or see the
   Egg Noodles and Wonton Wrappers
   recipe on page 11) .... 400 g (14 oz) packet
wonton wrappers (or see the
   Egg Noodles and Wonton Wrappers
   recipe on page 11) .... 200 g (7 oz) packet
spring onions (scallions) to garnish
some steamed vegetables to serve

KAI SUN

bicarbonate of soda
   (baking soda) .... 100 g (3½ oz)

BROTH

spring onions (scallions),
   trimmed and cut in half 4
piece of fresh ginger root,
   thinly sliced .... 2.5 cm (1 in)
sesame oil .... 1 teaspoon
garlic cloves, smashed 2
Shaoxing wine .... 2 tablespoons
chicken stock cubes 2
water .... 800 ml (27 fl oz/3½ cups)
sea salt and freshly ground black pepper

FILLING

spring onions (scallions), thinly sliced 3
Chinese leaf, finely chopped .... 100 g (3½ oz)
raw king prawns (shrimp), deveined
   and minced .... 200 g (7 oz)
minced (ground) pork .... 300 g (10½ oz)
cornflour (cornstarch) .... 2 teaspoons
sesame oil .... 2 teaspoons
Shaoxing wine .... 2 teaspoons
light soy sauce .... 2 teaspoons
salt and white pepper .... pinch
piece of fresh ginger root, crushed .... 40 g (½ oz)

METHOD

Put the bicarbonate of soda on a clean baking sheet and bake at 120°C fan (275°F/gas 1) for 1 hour. Leave to cool and store in an airtight container.

Make the broth by adding spring onion, ginger, sesame oil, garlic, Shaoxing wine, stock cubes, and salt and pepper (to taste) to a large saucepan and top up with the water. Let the broth bubble away and reduce to increase the intensity of the flavour (let it come to the boil, then put a lid on and simmer until ready to use). Taste for seasoning.

If making the noodles and wrappers from scratch, see the instructions on page 11.

For the filling, add the spring onions, Chinese leaf, prawns, pork, cornflour, sesame oil, Shaoxing wine, soy sauce, salt and pepper, and ginger to a bowl.

Put a small teaspoon of the filling in the middle of the square wonton wrapper, dampen the edge and fold over or pleat. Keep repeating until all the meat mixture has been used up.

Bring a saucepan of water to the boil, add the noodles and boil for about 2 minutes. Lift the noodles out with a slotted spoon and put in cold water to refresh them. Then divide the noodles between four bowls.

Bring the same saucepan of water to the boil again and add the wontons. Once they float to the top, after about 3 minutes, they are ready.

Add eight wontons to each bowl of noodles, top with the broth and some steamed vegetables, then garnish with spring onions.

Cheung Fun Noodle Bowl

This delicious dish can be found in Hong Kong street market carts and at dim sum restaurants, and is often called *joo cheung fun*, which literally translates as 'pig intestine noodles' because the rolled-up rice noodle looks like intestines! Not the most appetising description, I know, but I swear these are super delicious! They are served plain, with fillings or topped with peanut butter and hoisin sauce as I've served them here.

Serves: 2
Prep: 10 minutes
Cook: 20 minutes

INGREDIENTS

rice flour .... 120 g (4¼ oz/1 cup)
wheat starch .... 50 g (1¾ oz)
cornflour (cornstarch) .... 40 g (1½ oz)
salt .... ½ teaspoon
vegetable oil, plus
    extra for brushing .... 1 tablespoon

PEANUT BUTTER SAUCE

smooth peanut butter .... 1½ tablespoons
boiling water .... 4 tablespoons

SWEET SAUCE

light soy sauce .... 1½ tablespoons
granulated sugar .... 2 teaspoons
hoisin sauce .... 2 tablespoons
boiling water .... 2 tablespoons

TO SERVE

toasted white sesame seeds
thinly sliced spring onions (scallions)
Suzie's Chilli Oil (see page 48)

METHOD

Set up a steamer, half-fill the pan with water and bring to the boil over a high heat.

Make the two sauces: combine the peanut butter sauce ingredients in one bowl and the soy sauce ingredients in another. Set aside.

To make the rice noodle rolls, mix the rice flour, wheat starch, cornflour, salt and oil in a heatproof jug. Add 250 ml (8½ fl oz/1 cup) of boiling water and whisk. Keep whisking and slowly add 100 ml (3½ fl oz/scant ½ cup) lukewarm water, whisking continuously – you want the batter to have a thin soup texture and not be too thick (you may not need all the lukewarm water).

Brush a square or round, non-stick cake tin (pan) small enough to fit in your steamer with vegetable oil. Whisk the batter well and pour in enough to just cover the bottom of the tin. Using rubber gloves, put the tin into the steamer and swirl the mixture until it covers bottom completely. You do not want any holes or gaps. Put the lid on and steam for 2–3 minutes until the sheet of rice mixture is translucent, then take out of the steamer and leave to cool for a couple of minutes. Roll up the noodle using a spatula, and steam the rest of the batter in the same way, brushing the tin with more oil each time, until it's all used up.

Cut the noodle rolls into 5 cm (2 in) chunks (the batter should make approximately eight rolls of noodles) and top with the peanut butter and hoisin sauce, sesame seeds, spring onions and my chilli oil.

Crispy Seafood Noodles

My kids love this Chinese restaurant classic. The crunch of the noodles against the sweet seafood mix and vegetables is just a lovely combination – it is gobbled up in no time!

Serves: 4
Prep: 20 minutes
Cook: 15 minutes

INGREDIENTS

fine dried egg noodles .... 400 g (14 oz)
vegetable oil .... 4 tablespoons

SEAFOOD SAUCE

large spring onions (scallions),
    white and lighter green parts
    separated from the darker green pieces 4
vegetable oil .... 1 tablespoon
piece of ginger, thinly sliced .... 40 g (1½ oz)
crushed garlic .... 2 heaped teaspoons
oyster sauce .... 4–5 tablespoons
toasted sesame oil .... 1 teaspoon
chicken stock (made with 2 chicken
    stock cubes) .... 800 ml (27 fl oz/3½ cups)
Shaoxing wine .... 2 teaspoons
large carrot, peeled and
    thinly sliced diagonally 1
large handful of mushrooms, sliced
    (any variety) scallops, halved horizontally
    (so still a disc shape) .... 400 g (14 oz)
king prawns (shrip), peeled,
    deveined and butterflied .... 400 g (14 oz)
6 squid bodies, peeled and cross-hatched to
    create a diamond pattern (you can also use
    the tentacles) .... about 300 g (10½ oz)
cornflour (cornstarch) paste .... 2 teaspoons
sea salt and freshly ground black pepper

METHOD

Preheat the oven to 160°C fan (350°F/gas 4).

Prepare the noodles by placing them in a mixing bowl or saucepan. Pour boiling water over them and let them sit in the water for 10 minutes. Strain and rinse with cold water, then place on top of a colander and let dry for 10 minutes.

Heat the vegetable oil in a wok or large frying pan (skillet) over the highest heat. Add the noodles to the pan in a flat disc shape and fry for a couple of minutes (not stirring) until crispy underneath, then flip and repeat on the other side. Dab with paper towel and flip the disc of crispy noodles onto a large heatproof serving plate, then dab on the other side. Put into the oven to keep warm and crispy.

To make the seafood sauce, thinly slice the darker green lengths of spring onion lengthways and place in cold water – they will curl. Heat the vegetable oil in a wok or frying pan over a high heat, add the ginger, white/light green pieces of spring onion and garlic, then fry for about 1 minute until fragrant. Add the oyster sauce, sesame oil, chicken stock and Shaoxing wine and simmer for 2 minutes. Toss in the carrot and mushrooms and simmer for a further 2 minutes. Add the scallops, prawns and squid and cook for a maximum of 2 minutes, until the seafood is cooked. Add the cornflour paste to thicken the sauce. Taste and season accordingly, pour the seafood sauce over the crispy noodles and top with the green spring onion curls.

Veggie Singapore Noodles

Fun fact: Singapore noodles actually originate from Hong Kong, not Singapore. It is said that this dish was invented by chefs in the 1950s and '60s when trade was booming in Hong Kong and spices such as curry powders were readily accessible. The name was just to give the dish some flair.

This dish is on our Chinese takeaway menu and it is very popular! It is traditionally made with ham, chicken and prawns (shrimp) but I have made this veggie only, which tastes just as good.

Serves: 4
Prep: 10 minutes
Cook: 10 minutes

INGREDIENTS

vermicelli rice noodles .... 500 g (1 lb 2 oz)
   or dried noodles .... roughly 250 g (9 oz)
vegetable oil .... 4 tablespoons
large eggs, beaten with a pinch of salt 4
medium carrot, peeled and
   finely cut into matchsticks 1
sweet (bell) pepper (any colour),
   deseeded and thinly sliced 1
baby corn, thinly sliced diagonally 100 g (3½ oz)
mangetout (snow peas),
   thinly sliced diagonally .... 100 g (3½ oz)
medium onion, thinly sliced 1
curry powder (mild/medium/hot) .... 3 teaspoons
chilli powder (mild/medium/hot)
   (optional) .... 1 teaspoon
garlic powder/granules .... 1 teaspoon
light soy sauce .... 4 teaspoons
toasted sesame oil .... 2 teaspoons
sea salt and white pepper
spring onions (scallions), thinly sliced 2

METHOD

Soak the noodles in a heatproof bowl of boiling water for 1 minute, then strain and set aside.

Heat 2 tablespoons of the vegetable oil in a wok or frying pan (skillet) over a high heat, add the beaten eggs and fry for a minute on each side, without stirring, until they set like an omelette. Transfer to a plate, then cut into thin strips.

Heat 1 tablespoon of the oil in the wok or frying pan over a high heat, add the carrot, pepper, baby corn and mangetout with a splash of water to stop them burning and fry for a minute. Transfer to a plate. In the same wok or frying pan (you don't need to clean it) add the remaining tablespoon of oil, then add the onion with a splash of water, the curry powder, chilli powder (if using – I use mild curry powder and leave out the chilli powder when I'm cooking this for kids) and garlic powder or granules and fry for a couple of minutes over a high heat until the aromas are released. Toss in the cooked vermicelli and put all the vegetables back in the wok or pan. Toss again so everything is evenly distributed. Add the soy sauce, sesame oil and egg strips and keep frying and tossing until the noodles change to a golden yellow colour. Taste and season with salt and pepper as needed, add the spring onions and serve.

Duck and Pineapple Fried Rice

When we visited Hong Kong, we always went to a super fancy Vietnamese restaurant called The Golden Bull in Tsim Sha Tsui with my Auntie Cindy's family. On our family's takeaway menu there is a duck and pineapple sauce dish with fried rice. One day my mum made this dish in a dry-fried rice format and it was delicious.

Serves: 4
Prep: 10 minutes
Cook: 10 minutes

INGREDIENTS

pineapple, finely diced (preferably fresh)	175 g (6 oz)
vegetable oil	1 tablespoon
medium onion, thinly sliced	1
grated fresh ginger root	1 tablespoon
grated garlic	1 teaspoon
shredded duck or thinly sliced cooked duck	200 g (7 oz)
cooked basmati rice	400 g (14 oz)
chicken stock powder	½ teaspoon
Shaoxing wine	½ tablespoon
light soy sauce	½ tablespoon
oyster sauce	1 tablespoon
peas	handful
sea salt and freshly ground black pepper	

METHOD

If you are using a fresh pineapple to present the dish, carefully cut it in half lengthways. Cut around the edges, leaving a 1 cm (½ in) gap between the outer edge and the flesh (make sure you don't slice straight through the skin). Cut down either side of the core and remove it, then carefully score the flesh in a grid pattern so you can extract cubes of the pineapple with a spoon or knife. Then finely dice.

Heat the vegetable oil in a wok or frying pan (skillet) over a high heat. Add the onion, ginger and garlic and fry for a few minutes until fragrant, being careful to prevent the vegetables burning, and adding a splash of water if they catch. Add the duck and fry for another minute, then add the basmati rice and chicken stock powder and toss everything together using a wooden spoon, frying for 5 minutes until piping hot and making sure there are no lumps of rice. Add the Shaoxing wine, light soy sauce and oyster sauce and mix, then add the peas and pineapple and mix well. Taste and season. Serve in the hollowed-out pineapple halves (if you used a fresh pineapple) or a large dish.

ALL-IN-ONE DISHES

Here are a few recipes that are cooked in one vessel and are bursting with flavour. Some of them are slow-cooked dishes my mum used to make for us when she had time to plan ahead, but I have also included some super-quick and nutritious ones that I have been making myself for years.

CHAPTER SIX

CHINESE BEEF BRISKET	**90**
STEWED PORK RIBS WITH POTATOES AND BUTTERNUT SQUASH	**92**
STEAMED EGGS	**94**
QUORN AND CASHEW NUT STIR-FRY	**95**
***CHAR SIU* CHICKEN FILLETS**	**96**

Chinese Beef Brisket

This is a Hong Kong food market staple! When we were younger there was never a time we did not go for *ngau lam mein* (beef belly noodles). *Ngau lam* is one of those traditional Chinese 'casseroles' originally made with beef flank (skirt), which is found in the underbelly of the cow. It has layers of sinew and tendons which can potentially make it tough, but when slow-cooked it just melts in the mouth. This recipe uses beef brisket, which is easier to source than beef flank. I have also swapped out the Chinese radish (aka daikon/mooli) that's typically used in the dish for carrots.

Serves: 6
Prep: 10 minutes
Cook: 3 hours 15 minutes

INGREDIENTS

beef brisket, cut into large chunks .... about 1 kg (2 lb 4 oz)
vegetable oil .... 2 tablespoons
piece of fresh ginger root, sliced .... 40 g (1½ oz)
Shaoxing wine (or cooking sake /mirin/dry sherry) .... 250 ml (8½ fl oz/1 cup)
light soy sauce .... 3 tablespoons
dark soy sauce .... 2 tablespoons
oyster sauce .... 2 tablespoons
Chinese five-spice powder .... 2 tablespoons
garlic cloves 3
star anise 2
bay leaves 2
brown sugar .... 1 tablespoon
large carrots (about 750 g/1 lb 10 oz), peeled and cut diagonally into chunks 6
spring onions (scallions), cut into 2.5 cm (1 in) pieces and smashed 3
cornflour (cornstarch) paste (optional) .... 2 teaspoons
sea salt and white pepper

METHOD

Put the chunks of beef in a large saucepan and cover with about 1 litre (34 fl oz/4 cups) of cold water. Bring to the boil, then boil for 10–15 minutes, skimming off the impurities or scum that float on the surface with a large spoon. Remove the meat with a slotted spoon and place in a bowl. Keep the liquid the beef was boiled in.

Heat the vegetable oil in the same large pan over a high heat, add the ginger and fry for a couple of minutes until fragrant.

Add the Shaoxing wine, soy sauces, oyster sauce, Chinese five-spice powder, cloves, star anise, bay leaves and brown sugar and let everything bubble for a couple of minutes, then return the beef to the pan and toss it in the sauce. Pour enough of the reserved beef cooking liquid over the meat to cover (about 600 ml/ 20 fl oz/2½ cups). To cook on the stovetop, reduce the heat, cover with a lid and simmer for 2 hours 45 minutes to 3 hours until the meat melts in your mouth.

Add the carrots and more of the beef stock liquid to cover everything (if needed), then put the lid on. Increase the heat to medium and cook for about 15 minutes until the carrots are soft. Add the spring onions. Taste and season accordingly. If you like a thick sauce, add the cornflour paste and bring to the boil. If the flavour is too intense, add water and let it bubble away for another 5 minutes. Fish out the cloves, star anise and bay leaves and serve with rice or noodles.

TOP TIP

The leftover beef stock will keep in the fridge for four days or in the freezer for a month, and can be used to make broths for noodle bowls or Mum's Oxtail Soup (see page 156).

Stewed Pork Ribs with Potatoes and Butternut Squash

Mum made this dish with the ribs and potatoes, as I have here, or with chicken wings, both of which are perfect for this stew. You could also use pork chops or pork belly cut into chunks. My big sister Angela adds butternut squash, which gives the dish more sweetness and texture, and incorporates more good veg in our meal!

Serves: 4
Prep: 10 minutes
Cook: 1 hour

INGREDIENTS

pork ribs .... about 500 g (1 lb 2 oz)
vegetable oil .... 4 tablespoons
large potatoes, peeled and cut
    into large cubes .... 4 (about 500 g/1 lb 2 oz)
piece of fresh ginger root, sliced .... 30 g (1 oz)
large spring onions (scallions), cut into 5 cm
    (2 in) lengths (paler parts intact for
    frying and green parts to garnish) 3
garlic cloves, bashed 4
light soy sauce .... 3 tablespoons
caster (superfine) sugar .... 1 teaspoon
toasted sesame oil .... 1 teaspoon
Shaoxing wine .... 1 tablespoon
ground white pepper .... large pinch
butternut squash, deseeded, peeled
    and diced .... 300 g (10½ oz)
cornflour (cornstarch) paste
    (optional) .... 2 teaspoons
sea salt and freshly ground black pepper

METHOD

Put the ribs in a large saucepan with enough cold water to cover. Bring to the boil, then boil for about 5 minutes, skimming off the impurities or scum that float on the surface with a large spoon. Remove the meat with a slotted spoon and place in a bowl. Keep the liquid the ribs were boiled in.

In the same pan, fry the potatoes in batches in some oil over a medium heat to seal and brown on all sides. Lift the potatoes out into a bowl and set aside.

In the same pan, heat a couple of tablespoons of oil over a high heat, add the ginger, pale spring onion stalks and garlic and fry for a couple of minutes until fragrant, watching to make sure they don't burn. Add the soy sauce, sugar, sesame oil, Shaoxing wine and white pepper and stir. Add the ribs, then the fried potatoes, and add enough of the pork rib cooking stock to cover everything (400 ml/13 fl oz/1½ cups). Cover and simmer for 15 minutes.

Add the butternut squash and simmer for another 40 minutes. Check on the ribs, and if the meat is starting to come away from the bones, then it is ready. Taste and season as required – you may want to add a dash more soy sauce. Add water if you want more sauce, or if you want it thicker, add the cornflour paste a teaspoon at a time and allow it to come to the boil after each addition until it reaches your desired thickness. Garnish with the spring onion greens and serve.

Steamed Eggs

Mum used to make these silky steamed eggs with so many different ingredients, including minced (ground) pork, prawns (shrimp), spring onions (scallions), dried shrimp and mushrooms, to name but a few. This is a great recipe to use up whatever you have to hand and it lends itself well to so many flavours. Simply add any extra ingredients once you have strained the eggs.

Serves: 4
Prep: 5 minutes
Cook: 20 minutes

INGREDIENTS

EGG MIXTURE

large eggs 4
vegetable or chicken stock,
    slightly cooled .... 300–400 ml (13 fl oz/
    generous 1½ cups)
ground white pepper .... ¼ teaspoon
salt .... pinch

GARNISH

spring onions (scallions), thinly sliced
light soy sauce
sesame oil

METHOD

Set up a steamer, half-fill the pan with water and bring to the boil over a high heat. Put the top steamer section on the bottom section or set up a stand in the large pan to act like a steamer.

Crack the eggs into a measuring jug, then add 1.5–2 times of stock to the volume of the eggs (so if the eggs are sitting at 200 ml/7 fl oz, add 300–400 ml/13 fl oz stock; the higher the proportion of stock to egg, the silkier the dish will be). Add the white pepper and salt to the jug and mix.

Switch off the heat for the steamer (you do not want to scald yourself, but you have to work quickly at this point). Put a heatproof dish or bowl in the steamer (or on the stand), then put a fine sieve over the heatproof dish or bowl and pour the egg mixture through. This removes any lumps and air bubbles. Cover the dish or bowl with foil or cling film (plastic wrap) so water droplets do not disrupt the surface of the steamed eggs. Return the steamer to a medium heat (if it is too hot, it will curdle the eggs) and steam for 10–15 minutes, depending on the size of the heatproof dish. The eggs will have the consistency of wobbly jelly when they are ready. Garnish with the spring onions, soy sauce and sesame oil.

Quorn and Cashew Nut Stir-fry

This quick, all-in-one stir-fry mashes up key Chinese flavours with Western ingredients, including Mediterranean veg, which I always seem to have in abundance in my fridge! Using a meat alternative is a great way to add extra protein to this dish, too.

Serves: 4
Prep: 5 minutes
Cook: 10 minutes

INGREDIENTS

vegetable oil ....2 tablespoons
medium onion, thinly sliced 1
large garlic cloves, sliced 2
light soy sauce ....2 tablespoons
oyster sauce ....2 tablespoons
toasted sesame oil ....1 teaspoon
sweet (bell) pepper, deseeded
    and thinly sliced 1
courgette (zucchini), halved lengthways
    then sliced diagonally 1
cornflour (cornstarch) paste
    (optional) ....2 teaspoons
quorn ....250 g (9 oz)
sea salt and ground white pepper
handful of cashew nuts, toasted in a dry pan,
    to garnish

METHOD

Heat the vegetable oil in a wok or frying pan (skillet) over a high heat, add the onion, garlic and a splash of water and fry for a couple of minutes until lightly golden, being careful not to let the vegetables burn.

Add the soy sauce, oyster sauce and sesame oil and let everything bubble away for a couple of minutes, then toss in the pepper and courgette and simmer for a further 5 minutes. Taste and season as required, maybe adding some extra soy sauce.

If you want the sauce to be thicker, add the cornflour paste, then finally add the quorn and make sure it is covered in the sauce. Cook for about 5 minutes until the quorn is heated through (it may take less or more time, depending on whether it is frozen or not). Garnish with the cashew nuts and serve with noodles or rice.

Char Siu Chicken Fillets

A spin on the traditional *char siu* pork, this is a quick and easy version using chicken mini fillets – perfect for little fingers!

Serves: 4
Prep: 5 minutes, plus minimum 5 minutes' marinating time (ideally overnight)
Cook: 10 minutes

INGREDIENTS

chicken mini fillets .... 500 g (1 lb 2 oz)

CHAR SIU MARINADE

black treacle .... 15 g (½ oz)
brown sugar .... 10 g (¼ oz)
honey .... 25 g (1 oz)
hoisin sauce .... 30 g (1 oz)
dark soy sauce .... 10 g (¼ oz)
Chinese five-spice powder .... 1 teaspoon
vegetable oil .... ½ tablespoon
oyster sauce .... 20 g (¾ oz)
red food colouring .... 1 teaspoon

METHOD

Place a bowl on a set of scales, then put a sandwich bag in the bowl and measure all the ingredients for the marinade directly into the bag. Add the chicken mini fillets and swish the marinade around the fillets. Put the bag flat on a baking tray (pan) so the maximum amount of marinade is surrounding the meat and leave for at least 5 minutes, but for even better results keep in the fridge overnight.

Turn your grill to high and line the grill tray with foil. Place the marinated chicken pieces on the tray and baste them with the marinade from the bag using a pastry brush. Grill for about 5 minutes on each side until cooked through and slightly charred.

TOP TIPS

Using a sandwich bag on top of the scales to measure the marinade ingredients directly into cuts down on washing up!

Use the leftover marinade to coat chicken wings.

Use this chicken as a substitute for pork in the *Char Siu, Green Bean and Egg Hash* (page 111).

QUICK MIDWEEK MEALS

The majority of these speedy meals were originally made by my mum and now I am making them for my little ones. The thought that I am passing these dishes on to my family is very comforting.

CHAPTER SEVEN

KETCHUP FRANKFURTERS	100
BEEF, BLACK PEPPER AND ASPARAGUS	103
EGG AND TOMATO	104
MA PO TOFU WITH AUBERGINE	106
COLD SESAME AND PEANUT NOODLES	108
CHAR SIU, GREEN BEAN AND EGG HASH	111

Ketchup Frankfurters

This may seem like a very unconventional dish, but the frankfurters are super tasty and it is a brilliantly simple recipe. Mum would have served this at breakfast with eggs, or with rice or noodles for lunch or dinner.

Serves: 4
Prep: 5 minutes
Cook: 5 minutes

INGREDIENTS

vegetable oil .... 1 teaspoon
frankfurters, cut into 2.5 cm (1 in) chunks 10
tomato ketchup .... 4 tablespoons
runny honey .... 1½ tablespoons
toasted sesame oil .... ½ teaspoon
sea salt and freshly ground black pepper
    (optional)
white or black sesame seeds, to serve

METHOD

Heat the vegetable oil in a frying pan (skillet) over a high heat, add the frankfurters and fry for 3 minutes until they have browned and shrunk a little. Add the ketchup, honey and a splash of water and toss for a couple of minutes, letting the mixture become sticky around all the frankfurters. Drizzle with the sesame oil and toss to mix.

Taste and if you think the sausages need more seasoning, add a little bit more ketchup (for tang), honey (for sweetness) or salt and pepper.

Sprinkle with sesame seeds and serve.

TOP TIP

If you don't have frankfurters, cooked cocktail sausages work really well, too.

Beef, Black Pepper and Asparagus

This dish was a go-to for my mum in asparagus season (spring). Mum loved learning about the health benefits of certain foods and I remember her telling us that asparagus was very good for the digestive system. And so yet again, another vegetable was added to the long list of others that were 'very good' for us. Not that we needed convincing ... we ate everything that was put in front of us!

Serves: 4
Prep: 10 minutes, plus minimum 10 minutes' marinating time
Cook: 10 minutes

INGREDIENTS

rump steak, thinly sliced
   against the grain .... 500 g (1 lb 2 oz)
asparagus spears, trimmed and
   cut into large chunks .... 250 g (9 oz)
vegetable oil .... 2 tablespoons
cornflour (cornstarch) paste
   (optional) .... 2 teaspoons

MARINADE

light soy sauce .... 2 teaspoons
dark soy sauce .... 2 teaspoons
sesame oil .... 1 teaspoon
Shaoxing wine .... 2 teaspoons
cornflour (cornstarch) .... 1 teaspoon

BLACK PEPPER SAUCE

vegetable oil .... 1 tablespoon
large garlic clove, finely chopped or grated 1
white ground pepper .... ½ teaspoon
coarse ground black pepper .. 1 teaspoon
light soy sauce .... 1 tablespoon
Shaoxing wine .... 1 teaspoon
oyster sauce .... 2 teaspoons
toasted sesame oil .... 1 teaspoon
chicken stock .... about 200 ml
   (7 fl oz/scant 1 cup)

METHOD

Put the steak in a bowl, add all the marinade ingredients and mix to coat. Leave to marinate for at least 10 minutes (the marinade can be covered and kept in the fridge up to a day ahead).

Cook the asparagus spears in a wok or saucepan of boiling water for 2 minutes, then drain and rinse under cold water straight away to stop them cooking – you want them to remain crunchy.

Heat the vegetable oil in a wok or frying pan (skillet) over a high heat, add the marinated beef strips and fry for a couple of minutes – do not overcook them (pink is fine). Remove from the wok or pan.

Now make the black pepper sauce. Add the vegetable oil to the wok or frying pan (you don't need to clean it), place over a high heat, then add the garlic and fry for about 30 seconds, just until it starts to release its aromas. Add the white pepper, black pepper, soy sauce, Shaoxing wine, oyster sauce and sesame oil and simmer for a couple of minutes, then add the stock until the sauce reaches your desired thickness. Taste and season as required. Add water or extra stock if you want more sauce, or if you want it thicker add 1 teaspoon of cornflour paste at a time and allow it to come to the boil after each addition. Return the beef and asparagus to the wok or frying pan and serve.

TOP TIP

Green beans or tenderstem broccoli work well as a substitute when asparagus isn't in season.

Egg and Tomato

This is the ultimate Chinese comfort food, a dish that is cooked in many Chinese households as it uses simple everyday ingredients which you probably already have in your fridge or larder. Mum made this dish at least once a week and I now love making it for my little ones, serving it alongside a big bowl of rice.

Serves: 4
Prep: 5 minutes
Cook: 10 minutes

INGREDIENTS

vegetable oil ....2 tablespoons
medium eggs, beaten 6
large onion, sliced 1
large tomatoes, cut into wedges 4
   (about 500 g/1 lb 2 oz)
tomato ketchup ....5 tablespoons
caster (superfine) sugar ....1 heaped teaspoon
sea salt and ground white pepper
large spring onion (scallion), thinly sliced
   diagonally, to garnish 1

METHOD

Heat the vegetable oil in a wok or frying pan (skillet) over a medium heat, add the beaten eggs and cook for 5 minutes until lightly set like an omelette – you don't want the egg crispy, just lightly cooked. Set aside on a plate.

In the same pan, heat the oil over a high heat. Add the onion and a splash of water and cook for a couple of minutes until softened, then add the tomatoes and cook for a few more minutes – you want them to become nice and soft as well, as they form the sauce. Add the ketchup and sugar and let everything bubble away for 5 minutes until the sauce has slightly thickened. Add a pinch each of salt and white pepper, taste and add more seasoning if necessary. Finally, toss the eggs into the wok or pan and break them up with a wooden spoon, mixing them through the tomato sauce. Garnish with the spring onion and serve with rice.

Ma Po Tofu with Aubergine

Ma Po Tofu is a spicy beef or pork mince dish from the Sichuan province of China and should be a tongue-numbing experience. When Mum made it, it had a slight kick and was a delight to eat with rice. Here, I use my homemade chilli oil which gives just the right amount of heat. My sister Veronica inspired me to add aubergine (eggplant) – I love adding veggies to my dishes wherever I can!

Serves: 2
(large portions)
Prep: 10 minutes
Cook: 10 minutes

INGREDIENTS

vegetable oil ....1 tablespoon
Suzie's Chilli Oil (page 48)
   or shop-bought alternative
   (optional) ....1 teaspoon
garlic, crushed or grated ....2 large cloves
piece of fresh ginger root, grated .....20 g (¾ oz)
red chilli, thinly sliced (or more
   if you like it spicier) ....10 g (¼ oz)
chilli bean paste/sauce
   (*toban djan*) ....1½ tablespoons
small aubergine (eggplant), sliced or cubed 1
minced (ground) beef or pork   400 g (14 oz)
vegetable stock
   or water ......about 150 ml (5 fl oz/scant ⅔ cup)
cornflour (cornstarch) paste ....2 teaspoons
white pepper ....pinch
silken tofu, cubed ....300 g (10½ oz)
sea salt
large spring onions (scallions),
   sliced, to garnish 2

METHOD

Heat the vegetable oil in a wok or frying pan (skillet) over a high heat, add the chilli oil (if using) and the garlic, ginger and chilli and fry for about 1 minute until fragrant, then add the chilli bean paste/sauce and fry for a further minute. Add the aubergine and fry it in the spicy paste for about 5 minutes, then add the minced beef or pork and enough stock or water to just cover it and create a sauce. Break up the mince with a wooden spoon, then let it simmer away for 5 minutes before adding the cornflour paste to thicken the sauce, allowing it to come to the boil. If you would like the sauce even thicker, add more paste. Taste and season according to preference. Add the tofu and simmer for a further couple of minutes, then garnish with the spring onions and serve.

TOP TIPS

Transform this into a vegetarian dish by substituting the minced (ground) beef or pork for quorn mince.

The chilli bean paste (*toban djan*) can be used as a condiment or in noodles or marinades. Adding the chilli bean paste to hoisin sauce can make the base sauce for *kung po* dishes.

106

Cold Sesame and Peanut Noodles

This cold noodle dish is a real crowd-pleaser and is even better as leftovers. I always make extra to have for lunch the next day.

Serves: 4
(large portions)
Prep: 5 minutes
Cook: 5 minutes

INGREDIENTS

dried rice or glass noodles ....500 g (1 lb 2 oz)
unsalted peanuts ....handful
black or white sesame seeds ....handful

BASE SAUCE

smooth peanut butter ....100 g (3½ oz)
sesame paste (tahini) ....50 g (1¾ oz)
toasted sesame oil ....2 tablespoons
salt ....½ teaspoon
light soy sauce ....1½ tablespoons
rice wine vinegar ....2 tablespoons
white pepper ....½ teaspoon
vegetable stock powder ....1 teaspoon

VEGETABLES

Suzie's Pickled Veg (see page 72),
    thinly sliced ....200 g (7 oz)

OR

medium carrot, peeled and cut
    into matchsticks 1
green (bell) pepper, sliced into matchsticks 1
sea salt and white pepper
spring onions (scallions), thinly sliced
    diagonally, to serve 2

METHOD

Bring a large saucepan of water to the boil, add the rice or glass noodles and bring back to the boil for another 2 minutes. Strain the noodles using a colander and save at least 100 ml (3½ fl oz/scant ½ cup) of the noodle water, then rinse the strained noodles under cold running water until they are cool and set to one side.

Put the peanuts and sesame seeds in a dry, clean frying pan (skillet) and toast for a couple of minutes over a medium heat until they are lightly browned and toasted. Remove from the pan and set aside.

Now make the base sauce. Put the sauce ingredients in a bowl and whisk until smooth, then add 100 ml (3½ fl oz/scant ½ cup) of the reserved hot noodle water and the vegetable stock powder to the sauce, whisk again and taste: if the sauce is really thick, add more noodle water. It should be tangy and quite rich in flavour because of the peanut butter and sesame paste.

Then throw the pickled veg (or the carrot and pepper) and spring onions into the sauce. Add the noodles and toss. Taste and adjust to your liking, adding more rice wine vinegar for sharpness or salt and pepper or even more peanut butter or sesame paste. Finish with the toasted peanuts and sesame seeds and serve.

TOP TIP

The base sauce will keep in a jar in the fridge for at least a week and is delicious added to noodles or used as a salad dressing, or to spice up a coleslaw recipe instead of using mayo.

Char Siu, Green Bean and Egg Hash

This dish was my mum's very own special creation; it may not look like much, but it is really tasty! I thought this was a normal Chinese household dish but have discovered that my mum merged two dishes together – leftover barbecue pork (*char siu*) thrown in with green beans and eggs to make the perfect family dish. It ticks all the boxes for a mum feeding her little ones.

Serves: 4
Prep: 5 minutes
Cook: 10 minutes

INGREDIENTS

green beans, cut into small pieces ... 200 g (7 oz)
vegetable oil .... 2 tablespoons
char siu (barbecue) pork,
    cut into 1 cm (½ in) chunks .... 150 g (5 oz)
light soy sauce .... 1½ tablespoons
large eggs, beaten 5
toasted sesame oil .... 1 teaspoon
sea salt and white pepper

METHOD

Pour 100 ml (3½ fl oz/scant ½ cup) of water into a wok or frying pan (skillet), then add the chopped green beans. Bring the water to the boil, cover and let the green bean pieces steam over a high heat for about 2 minutes until they are just cooked. Remove the lid and let any extra water evaporate (if it hasn't done so already). Push the green beans to one side of the wok or frying pan and add 1 tablespoon of the oil, then add the *char siu* and fry for a couple of minutes. Add the light soy sauce and let everything bubble for about 30 seconds, then add the second tablespoon of oil and toss everything together. Now add the beaten eggs and sesame oil and cook for about 30 seconds so they have 'set' a bit, then flip chunks of the mixture over to cook the other side. It will be fully cooked in a couple of minutes. Season to taste and get ready to eat!

TOP TIP

This recipe can be made using plain cooked chicken, ham or even spam!

FAMILY FAVOURITES

This selection of recipes is a snapshot of what I feed my family on a regular basis. All the dishes are devoured by my children!

CHAPTER EIGHT

BEEF *HO FUN* NOODLES	114
HONG KONG-STYLE CHICKEN WINGS	117
INSTANT NOODLE BOWL	118
TEA EGGS	121
KING PRAWNS, CELERY AND CARROT	123
MIXED VEGGIE EGG-FRIED RICE	124
CANTONESE STEAMED BLACK BEAN, GINGER AND SPRING ONION SALMON	126
XO SAUCE UDON NOODLES	128

Beef *Ho Fun* Noodles

This is a flat rice noodle dish which was always ordered when I went out for dim sum with my family when I was growing up. It was one of those dishes the whole family dived into when it arrived at the table. Tender marinated beef with chewy, flat rice noodles is nostalgia on a plate for me.

Serves: 4
Prep: 15 minutes
Cook: 25 minutes

INGREDIENTS

vegetable oil
rump steak, cut thinly
   against the grain .... 400 g (14 oz)
spring onions (scallions),
   white parts cut into 5-cm
   (2-in) long pieces and then
   in half lengthways 5
medium onion finely sliced 1
fresh ginger root, finely sliced
   into strips ½ thumb-sized piece (20 g/ ¾ oz)
garlic cloves, crushed 2
beansprouts .... 200 g

MARINADE

light soy sauce .... 2 tablespoons
dark soy sauce .... 1 teaspoon
sesame oil .... 1 teaspoon
cornflour (cornstarch) .... 1 teaspoon
Shaoxing wine (or white wine
   or cider vinegar) .... 1 tablespoon

NOODLES

rice flour .... 270 g (10 oz/1¾ cups)
cornflour (cornstarch) .... 160 g (5 oz/1 cup)
water .... 700 ml (24 fl oz/scant 3 cups)
oil

SAUCE

light soy sauce .... 5 tablespoons
dark soy sauce .... 2 tablespoons
sugar .... 1 teaspoon
black vinegar (or cider vinegar) .... 1 teaspoon
sea salt and white pepper

METHOD

Marinate the beef for at least 15 minutes (you can leave it covered overnight in the fridge as well).

To make the rice noodles, add the rice flour, cornflour and water to a bowl and whisk to form a batter. Transfer the batter to a large jug, then pour it into a 20 cm (8 in) greased tray (pan). Place the tray in a steamer, cover and steam for 3–5 minutes. Remove the tray carefully and, using a spatula, run it around the edge to peel away the sheet of batter. Lightly brush the batter with oil, then stack and use a sharp knife to cut into 2 cm (¾ in) strips to make the noodles.

Fry off the beef in a little vegetable oil in a wok or frying pan (skillet) in batches for a couple of minutes (rare/medium is fine). Remove and put the beef aside (do not clean the pan).

Add a little bit more oil if there is none left in the pan. Then fry off the spring onions and onions and add about 2 tablespoon of water, cooking for a couple of minutes until the water has evaporated and the onions have softened.

Add the ginger and garlic. Fry for a couple of minutes until fragrant. Then add the noodles and the sauce, and quickly toss for a couple more minutes until the noodles are soft.

Add the beansprouts and then the steak and cook for another couple of minutes. Taste and season to your liking. Then the noodles are ready to serve.

TOP TIP

I have simplified how to make the rice noodles from scratch but this dim sum classic will take you minutes to make if you use shop-bought noodles. Use 800 g (1 lb 12 oz) of fresh *ho fun* noodles.

Hong Kong-style Chicken Wings

Barbecuing is a big thing in Hong Kong, and during our summer holidays there we would have had at least one trip to a 'BBQ site'! Chicken wings are a weekly favourite in our household. My children absolutely love them. This is such an easy but delicious recipe which makes the most of simple ingredients.

Serves: 4
Prep: 10 minutes
Cook: 15 minutes

INGREDIENTS

chicken wings _____ 500 g (1 lb 2 oz)
toasted sesame oil _____ 1 teaspoon
light soy sauce _____ 3 tablespoons
runny honey, plus extra
    for brushing _____ 3 tablespoons
garlic powder/granules _____ ½ tablespoon
vegetable oil _____ 1 teaspoon
salt and white pepper _____ pinch of each

METHOD

Preheat the oven to 160°C fan (350°F/gas 4) and line a baking tray with baking parchment. Alternatively, prepare a barbecue.

Put the wings in a saucepan, cover with cold water and bring to the boil, then boil for 5 minutes, skimming off the impurities or scum that float on the surface with a large spoon. Use a slotted spoon to remove the wings and keep the chicken broth for other uses (see Top Tips below).

While the chicken is parboiling, put the sesame oil, soy sauce, honey, garlic, oil and salt and pepper in a bowl. Transfer the drained wings to this bowl and toss them to coat with the marinade, then let them sit for about 5 minutes to absorb all the flavours. The wings can also be left covered overnight in the refrigerator.

If you're baking the wings in the oven, put them on the lined baking tray and bake for 10 minutes, then remove the tray and brush with the juices and marinade from the bottom of the tray. Drizzle and brush with extra honey and roast for a further 5 minutes. If you're barbecuing the wings, baste them with more honey, place them on the grill and cook for 5–8 minutes on each side until slightly charred.

Check the wings are thoroughly cooked by cutting into them. If they aren't yet cooked through, roast for another 5 minutes.

TOP TIPS

Parboiling the wings before you barbecue or oven-bake them keeps them super juicy.

Do not throw out the water used to parboil the chicken wings. Instead, use it for stock or broths, such as the *Instant Noodle Bowl* (see overleaf).

Instant Noodle Bowl

This is a great way to use up the leftovers you have in your kitchen, whether it's things from your fridge or a random selection of ingredients like eggs, cooked meats (such as *char siu*, wings, ham), pickled veg (or regular veg), seeds/nuts, and so on. The instant noodles you need here are usually labelled as instant ramen noodles.

Serves: 1
Prep: 10 minutes
Cooks: 5 minutes

INGREDIENTS

dried instant ramen noodles .... 1 packet
    (about 100g/3½ oz)
light soy sauce .... ½ tablespoon
Suzie's Chilli Oil (see page 48) or a
    shop-bought chilli oil (optional) .... ½ teaspoon
garlic powder/granules .... ¼ teaspoon
onion powder .... ¼ teaspoon
chicken or vegetable stock
    (I usually have frozen chicken stock
    to hand, perhaps from the boiled
    wings on the previous page,
    but you can use a cube or
    powder instead) .... 200–400 ml (7–13 fl oz/
    scant 1 cup–generous 1½ cups)
toasted sesame oil .... 1 teaspoon
white pepper and salt

TOPPING IDEAS

boiled or fried eggs
leftover cooked meat
steamed vegetables
    or *Suzie's Pickled Vegetables* (page 72)
grated vegetables
sesame seeds
dried seaweed

METHOD

Cook the noodles according to the instructions on the packet, but for a minute less (no more than 3 minutes), then rinse under cold running water immediately after straining them. The instructions will not suggest rinsing the noodles but this stops them from going too mushy.

Put the light soy sauce, chilli oil (if using), garlic powder or granules and onion powder in a large serving bowl and mix to combine.

Bring the stock to the boil, add half to the serving bowl and mix. Place the noodles in the stock, toss, then season to taste. If you like more liquid, add more of the boiled stock. Arrange whatever you like on top: I don't think any bowl of instant noodles I have made has ever been the same, as I always have different things in my fridge and cupboards to put on top!

TOP TIP

My mum always believed in rinsing the noodles first and making a fresh broth for them as she said it made them taste better, and I think she was right!

Tea Eggs

The smell of these eggs is so reminiscent of Hong Kong. I have such fond memories of seeing them piled high in gigantic pots around street vendors' stalls and shops. They are sold as snacks but can be added to rice or noodle bowls, and also eaten hot or cold. My mum used to make big pots of these which never lasted long!

Makes: 6 tea eggs
Prep: 20 minutes, plus minimum 24 hours' marinating time
Cook: 50 minutes

INGREDIENTS

large eggs, cleaned 6

MARINADE

piece of fresh ginger root,
    cut into 2 slices .... 10 g (¼ oz)
star anise 2
ground cinnamon .... 2 teaspoons
bay leaves 2
strong tea bags 2
dark soy sauce .... 200 ml (7 fl oz/scant 1 cup)
caster (superfine) sugar .... 1 teaspoon
salt .... ½ teaspoon
Shaoxing wine .... 1 tablespoon
Chinese five spice powder ...... 1 heaped teaspoon
black peppercorns 5

METHOD

Bring a small saucepan of water to the boil, add the eggs and boil for 7 minutes, then plunge into cold water straight away to stop them cooking. Drain the eggs, then crack the shells gently (do not crack them so much that the shells peel away, just so they are cracked all over).

Throw out the water in the pan, then add all the marinade ingredients, including the cracked eggs, to the clean pan (make sure the eggs are submerged in the liquid). Bring to a gentle simmer and cook for 45 minutes, then remove from the heat and leave the eggs to cool in the pan. Pour everything into a bag and leave for at least 24 hours (or up to four days) in the fridge.

The eggs can be reheated in the marinade in a pan if you want to eat them hot.

King Prawns, Celery and Carrot

This is a very fresh dish my mum used to make for us as a family, which ticked all the boxes for feeding her kids, as it included lots of veggies and seafood. She often added scallops if she could get hold of them at the Tuesday fish market. Serve this with a bowl of basmati rice or noodles.

Serves: 4
Prep: 10 minutes
Cook: 10 minutes

INGREDIENTS

vegetable oil	1 tablespoon
small onion, thinly sliced	1
small celery sticks, thinly sliced diagonally	2
medium carrots, peeled, halved lengthways and thinly sliced diagonally	2
chicken stock powder	2 tablespoons
grated or crushed garlic	1 teaspoon
oyster sauce, plus extra if required	1 tablespoon
Shaoxing wine	1 tablespoon
king prawns (shrimp), peeled and deveined (you can butterfly them by slicing down the back of the prawn if you wish – see *Sweet and Spicy King Prawns* on page 32)	400 g (14 oz)
scallops, halved widthways (optional)	200 g (7 oz)
toasted sesame oil	1 teaspoon
cornflour (cornstarch) paste	2 teaspoons
sea salt and white pepper	
roasted cashew nuts, to garnish	large handful

METHOD

Heat the vegetable oil in a wok or frying pan (skillet) over a high heat, add the onion, celery and carrots and a large splash of water and sauté for a couple of minutes. Then add the chicken stock powder and mix it through the vegetables. Add the garlic and fry for a couple of minutes until fragrant, then add the oyster sauce and Shaoxing wine. Add the king prawns, scallops and sesame oil and toss, then cover with a lid or piece of foil and cook for 1 minute.

If you would like more sauce, add some water and another tablespoon of oyster sauce, then taste and season as required. If you prefer the sauce thicker, add the cornflour paste one teaspoon at a time, and bring to the boil after each addition, until the sauce thickens. Garnish with roasted cashew nuts and serve.

TOP TIP

Cutting everything the same size and thickness speeds up the cooking time, so this is definitely a dish made in minutes, especially when you have hungry children on the prowl!

Mixed Veggie Egg-fried Rice

Fried rice is one of my go-to dishes to use up leftover ingredients. It's also a great meal for my children as it allows me to add more vegetables to their diets.

Serves: 4
Prep: 10 minutes
Cook: 25 minutes

INGREDIENTS

vegetable oil .... 4 tablespoons
large eggs, beaten 4
small onion, thinly sliced 1
garlic cloves, finely chopped or grated 2
fresh ginger root, thinly sliced ....
      ½ thumb-sized piece (about 20 g/ ¾ oz)
toasted sesame oil, plus extra to serve 1
   teaspoon
cold cooked basmati rice .... 500 g (1 lb 2 oz)
light soy sauce, plus extra
   to serve .... 2 tablespoons
peas .... handful
medium carrot, peeled and
   thinly sliced 1
mangetout (snow peas),
   thinly sliced at an angle .... handful
baby corn, thinly sliced at an angle .... handful
oyster sauce or
   vegetarian stir-fry sauce .... 2 tablespoons

TO GARNISH

spring onions (scallions), finely sliced 2
red chilli, finely sliced 1

METHOD

Heat 2 tablespoons of the oil in a wok or frying pan (skillet) over a high heat, add the beaten eggs and fry like an omelette for a couple of minutes, removing from the heat and putting on a plate just before the egg is fully cooked and solid (it will keep cooking after it is removed from the heat).

Heat the remaining oil in the same wok or pan over a high heat, add the onions and fry for a couple of minutes until slightly soft, then add the garlic and ginger and the sesame oil. Add the cooked rice, cooking it for a few minutes and breaking it up with a wooden spoon, then add the soy sauce and the vegetables and toss for a couple of minutes over the heat. Add the egg to the wok or pan, break it into smaller pieces with a wooden spoon and cook for 5 minutes. Taste and adjust the seasoning, adding the oyster sauce and more soy sauce and sesame oil if required. Serve, garnished with spring onions and chilli.

TOP TIP

Frozen veg such as peas and sweetcorn are great additions to this dish.

Cantonese Steamed Black Bean, Ginger and Spring Onion Salmon

This is a real family favourite. My mum used to make it for us as it was quick and easy – cooked in 20 minutes – and really nutritious. My children love this dish and gobble it all up when I serve it with rice or noodles.

Serves: 4
Prep: 10 minutes, plus 15 minutes' soaking time
Cook: 15 minutes

INGREDIENTS

dried fermented black beans .... 2 tablespoons
small onion, thinly sliced 1
salmon fillet .... about 600 g (1 lb 5 oz)
fresh ginger root, finely sliced
    into matchsticks, plus optional extra to
    garnish .... 2 tablespoons (approx. 30 g/1 oz)
large garlic cloves, finely chopped or grated 2
light soy sauce .... 1 tablespoon
toasted sesame oil .... 1 teaspoon
white pepper .... pinch

GARNISH

spring onions (scallions), thinly sliced 2
vegetable oil, heated to
    boiling point .... ½ tablespoon

METHOD

Put the fermented black beans in a small heatproof bowl, cover with boiling water and leave to soak for 15 minutes.

Set up a steamer, half-fill the pan with water and bring to the boil over a high heat.

Choose a heatproof dish that will fit in the steamer and one that the fish will fit in as well. Spread the sliced onion out evenly in the dish, then place the salmon, skin side down, on top (you don't want the skin of the fish to touch the plate).

Mix the ginger, garlic, soy sauce, sesame oil and pepper in a bowl, then pour the mixture over the salmon. Spoon over the soaked black beans (discard the soaking liquid as it's super salty). Place a piece of baking parchment over the fish so the steam doesn't dilute the flavour.

Once the water in the steamer pot is boiling, place the plate of fish with the parchment paper in the steamer and put the lid on. Leave to steam for about 15 minutes, depending on the size of your fish fillet. Once the salmon has been cooking for 10 minutes, take the lid off the steamer pot (be very careful not to scald yourself) and garnish the salmon with the spring onions, and more ginger if you wish. Bring the vegetable oil to the boil in a small frying pan, then pour it over the spring onions – this will enhance the flavour even more as it will lightly 'fry' the onions. The smell will be amazing! Remove the garnished fish from the steamer. Now you are ready to serve.

TOP TIP

Steam vegetables on top of the salmon with a piece of baking parchment separating the two. This saves an extra pot being used.

XO Sauce Udon Noodles

XO sauce is a really luxurious ingredient. Legend has it that it was developed in the prestigious Peninsula Hotel in Kowloon, Hong Kong, by a chef using high-end seafood products. Even though it is named after Cognac, it does not have one drop of alcohol in it, rather the name is used to denote its high-quality ingredients. My mum used to make noodles with this sauce all the time as it is a quick way of adding flavour to any dish. Udon noodles are so easy to get hold of now, which is a bonus for me as I can create a quick dinner in minutes. The thick, chewy texture of these noodles is really moreish.

Serves: 2
Prep: 5 minutes
Cook: 15 minutes

INGREDIENTS

udon noodles .... 200 g (7 oz) packet
vegetable oil .... 1 tablespoon
medium onion, sliced 1
large mushrooms, thinly sliced 2
napa cabbage leaves, thinly sliced 2
carrot, peeled and thinly sliced or grated 1
XO sauce .... 1½ tablespoons
oyster sauce .... 1½ tablespoons
light soy sauce .... ½ tablespoon
toasted sesame oil .... 1 teaspoon
white pepper .... ¼ teaspoon
sea salt and white pepper
large spring onion (scallion), sliced,
    to garnish 1

METHOD

Bring a small saucepan of water to the boil, add the udon noodles, bring to the boil again and the noodle strands will separate. Drain in a colander and set to one side.

Heat the vegetable oil in a wok or frying pan (skillet) over a high heat, add the onion, mushrooms, cabbage and carrot and fry for a couple of minutes, then add a splash of water to help soften the vegetables. Move the vegetables to one side of the wok or pan, add the XO sauce to the empty part of the wok or pan and fry for a couple of minutes – this will make the chilli and aromatics come to life. Toss the vegetables in the XO sauce, then add the oyster sauce and soy sauce and mix. Add the noodles, toss, cover with a lid and cook for a minute to soften the noodles, then drizzle over the sesame oil and add the white pepper and mix. Season to taste and finish with the spring onion to garnish.

TAKEAWAYS

Our family takeaway, Man Lee, opened on 11 July, 1980, and it is still going strong. Having grown up in the takeaway business I have always been asked for our recipes ... So here, I am sharing a few of our favourites, some of which I have modified for the home cook.

CHAPTER NINE

VEGGIE SPRING ROLLS	**132**
KING PRAWN SESAME TOAST	**134**
HOT AND SOUR SOUP	**137**
CHICKEN AND SWEETCORN SOUP	**138**
SALTED CHILLI TOFU WITH PERFECT BASMATI RICE	**140**
CANTONESE-STYLE SWEET AND SOUR CHICKEN	**143**
BEEF AND BLACK BEAN SAUCE	**144**

Veggie Spring Rolls

Spring rolls are a staple in Northern Ireland takeaways, and they are super simple to make. Buying the separate ingredients to make them can easily become wasteful, so using a stir-fry pack of vegetables and odds and ends you have to hand can help to avoid waste, and making your own wrappers is cost-effective, too. You can even add ham or cooked chicken.

    The assembled (uncooked) rolls can be made ahead and frozen and cooked straight from the freezer the next time you are craving them.

Makes: 12-14
Prep: 20-30 minutes if making wrappers from scratch
Cook: 20 minutes

INGREDIENTS

vegetable oil, for frying
spring roll wrappers (or see the
    Spring Roll Wrapper recipe on
    page 12)..............500 g (1 lb 2 oz) packet

FILLING

vegetable oil........................2 tablespoons
garlic cloves, grated...............................3
piece of fresh ginger root, grated......20 g (¾ oz)
red chilli, finely chopped, plus extra to serve......1
dark soy sauce.......................3 teaspoons
cornflour (cornstarch)..............1 teaspoon
toasted sesame oil..................1 teaspoon
pack of stir-fry vegetables (onions, carrots,
    cabbage, bell peppers, beansprouts),
    chopped to the same size......300 g (10½ oz)
bamboo shoots, drained and thinly sliced
    lengthways (optional)......................handful
mushrooms (white/chestnut/shiitake/wood ear),
    thinly sliced......................100 g (3½ oz)
spring onion (scallion), thinly sliced.............1
toasted sesame seeds.............2 teaspoons
sea salt and white pepper

DIPPING SAUCE

black vinegar or
    rice wine vinegar..............2 tablespoons
caster (superfine) or
    granulated sugar..............1 teaspoon
dark soy sauce.......................1 tablespoon
sesame oil............................1 teaspoon
finely diced chilli (optional)
spring onion (scallion), finely diced......1 teaspoon

METHOD

To make the filling mixture, heat the vegetable oil in a wok or frying pan (skillet) over a high heat, add the garlic, ginger and chilli and fry for a couple of minutes, watching carefully to make sure the vegetables don't burn. Meanwhile, mix the soy sauce, cornflour and sesame oil in a bowl, add the mixture to the wok or frying pan and let it bubble for a couple of minutes. Add the chopped vegetables, bamboo shoots (if using) and mushrooms and cook for about 3 minutes. Taste and season, then tip the mixture into a baking tray (pan) to cool. Once cool, toss in the spring onion and sesame seeds.

To make the spring roll wrappers from scratch, follow the instructions on page 12.

Shape about 2 tablespoons of the filling mixture into a log shape, about 2.5 cm (1 in) from the bottom edge of the wrapper nearest to you, then fold the bottom edge over the mixture and then the right side and the left side to make an envelope (make sure it is tight at the sides and bottom before you start rolling it). The spring roll needs to be rolled tightly into a cylindrical shape to the furthest point away from you. Make a thick paste with flour and a little water, then seal the roll with the paste using your finger. Repeat until all the mixture has been used up – it should make 12–14 spring rolls. If there are any holes in the wrappers use the flour paste to seal. They can be frozen at this point, if you wish.

Pour enough oil into a large saucepan so it is double the height of the spring rolls. To test if the oil is ready for frying, use the handle of a wooden spoon: the oil should fizz around it immediately. Gently place about three spring rolls in the pan and fry for about 2 minutes on each side until golden brown. Remove and drain on paper towel.

Mix all the dipping sauce ingredients together in a bowl and serve with the spring rolls.

TOP TIP

A packet of ready-made wrappers will make 30 spring rolls. So either keep the remaining wrappers tightly sealed in the refrigerator ready to make more spring rolls later that week or chop up into little pieces, deep fry until brown and sprinkle on top of *Chicken Congee* (see page 67) to give it extra bite.

King Prawn Sesame Toast

Prawn toast is one of my favourite takeaway starters. I love the combination of the juicy prawns (shrimp) with the crispy bread and crunchy sesame seeds – it's such a flavour explosion. Prawn toast originated from Guangzhou (the largest Cantonese-speaking region in China) and is therefore a popular Hong Kong dish (as Cantonese is the predominant language in Hong Kong). There are many ways to make prawn toast: here I have pared it down to the basic method – I promise you it is super tasty.

Makes: 4 slices
Prep: 10 minutes
Cook: 15 minutes

INGREDIENTS

black sesame seeds	4 tablespoons
white sesame seeds	4 tablespoons
king prawns, peeled and deveined (divided into 200 g/7 oz and 100 g/3½ oz)	about 300 g (10½ oz)
cornflour (cornstarch)	3 teaspoons
grated fresh ginger root (or ground ginger)	1 teaspoon
toasted sesame oil	1 teaspoon
salt	½ teaspoon
sugar	pinch
white pepper	large pinch
spring onions (scallions), finely chopped	2
bread (stale white bread is best for this)	4 slices
vegetable oil, for frying	

METHOD

Sprinkle the sesame seeds onto a plate.

If you have a food processor, put 200 g (7 oz) of the prawns in the bowl of the food processor with the cornflour, ginger, sesame oil, salt, sugar, pepper and spring onions and pulse until they turn into a smooth paste. Add the last 100 g (3½ oz) of prawns and blitz for a couple of pulses.

If you do not have a food processor, use your biggest kitchen knife to chop up all the prawns, ginger and spring onions finely on a chopping board until they form a paste. Put this paste into a bowl and mix in the cornflour, sesame oil, salt, sugar and pepper.

Using a butter knife, spread a quarter of the mixture evenly all over the surface of a piece of bread. Dip the bread, prawn-paste side down, into the sesame seeds. Set aside and repeat with the rest of the prawn mixture and bread.

Heat about 4 tablespoons of vegetable oil in a frying pan (skillet) over a medium heat. Test if the oil is ready for frying with the handle of a wooden spoon: the oil should fizz around the spoon immediately. Add two pieces of the toast to the pan, sesame seed and prawn-side-down, and fry for 3–4 minutes until the prawns are cooked through, then flip and cook the bread for 2–3 minutes on the other side until golden. Transfer to a paper towel, add a little more oil to the pan and repeat with the remaining two slices. If you prefer, you can bake the prawn toasts instead of frying them (see Top Tips).

Cut into triangles and enjoy!

TOP TIPS

If using fresh prawns, these can be made in bulk and frozen before frying, saving you lots of time! You can fry or bake from frozen.

For a healthier option, bake the prawn toast in a 200°C fan (425°F/gas 7) oven for 10 minutes until golden all over.

Hot and Sour Soup

This quick and simple, heart-warming soup can be made in minutes, using what you already have to hand at home. This is a real favourite of mine. I love adding extra black vinegar to give it an even tangier edge. For a more 'authentic' version you can use shiitake mushrooms, thinly sliced wood ear mushrooms, dried lily flowers and thin slices of cooked pork shoulder or ham.

Serves: 4
Prep: 5 minutes
Cook: 15 minutes

INGREDIENTS

chicken or
    vegetable stock ....1 litre (34 fl oz/4 cups)
light soy sauce ....3½ tablespoons
black or rice wine
    vinegar ....100 ml (3½ fl oz/scant ½ cup)
garlic granules
    (or freshly grated garlic) ....1 teaspoon
ground ginger
    (or grated fresh ginger root) ....1 teaspoon
chilli powder (mild/medium/hot) ....1 teaspoon
white pepper ....large pinch
salt ....pinch
mushrooms, sliced ....100 g (3½ oz)
bamboo shoots, drained and
    thinly sliced lengthways ....100 g (3½ oz)
cooked ham/chicken/tofu,
    thinly sliced (optional) ....handful
rehydrated shiitake/wood ear mushrooms
    or lily flowers (optional) ....handful
cornflour (cornstarch) paste ....3 tablespoons
large eggs, beaten 2
large spring onions (scallions), thinly sliced
    diagonally, to garnish 2

METHOD

Put the stock in a saucepan, add the soy sauce, black or rice wine vinegar, garlic, ginger, chilli, white pepper and salt and bring to the boil, then add the fresh mushrooms, bamboo shoots and any meat or tofu, shiitake/wood ear mushrooms or lily flowers and simmer for a couple of minutes to heat through. Start by adding 2 tablespoons of cornflour paste, then bring to the boil. If the soup is not thick enough, add more paste, a teaspoon at a time, and let it come to the boil after each addition.

Using a wooden spoon, swirl the soup, then tip in the beaten eggs and keep stirring – this will give you flecks of egg through the soup. Toss in the spring onions, taste and add a little more vinegar if you want it more 'sour', or more chilli powder if you want it spicier.

TOP TIP

This is a great soup to make for an unexpected veggie guest. Just swap out the meat and use up any vegetables you have to hand.

Chicken and Sweetcorn Soup

So many people have asked me for a recipe for this soup. Here is an easy version of this takeaway classic which is made with a few easy-to-source ingredients.

Serves: 4
Prep: 5 minutes
Cook: 10 minutes

INGREDIENTS

chicken stock (homemade or shop-bought) or veg stock) .... 1 litre (34 fl oz/4 cups)
cornflour (cornstarch) paste .... 3 tablespoons
tin of sweetcorn, drained .... 200 g (7 oz)
cooked small chicken breasts (sliced up or cubed) or tofu 3
white pepper .... large pinch
salt .... pinch
toasted sesame oil .... 2 teaspoons
large eggs, beaten 3
spring onions (scallions), finely chopped 2

METHOD

Put the stock and 2 tablespoons of cornflour paste in a saucepan and bring to the boil. If the stock is not thick enough, add the last of the paste a teaspoon at a time, letting it come to the boil after each addition. Add the sweetcorn, chicken (or tofu), pepper, salt, and sesame oil and let the soup bubble for another couple of minutes to heat through.

Bring the soup to the boil again, and using a wooden spoon, swirl the soup, tip in the beaten eggs and keep stirring – this will give you flecks of egg through the soup. Finally toss in the spring onions. Taste and season according to preference.

TOP TIPS

For a veggie version, swap out the chicken for tofu, then add half a large tin of creamed sweetcorn to give it extra body and sweetness.

Salted Chilli Tofu with Perfect Basmati Rice

Chinese salted chilli is a spice mix made up of fresh chilli, pepper, salt and Chinese five-spice powder. It is everywhere at the moment, so what better way to serve it but with crispy tofu. I am also including a foolproof method for making the best basmati rice all in one pot.

Serves: 4
Prep: 10 minutes
Cook: 30 minutes

INGREDIENTS

basmati rice................................200 g (7 oz/1 cup)
vegetable oil
onion, sliced...1
green (bell) pepper, deseeded and sliced.............1
large garlic clove, finely grated.............................1
grated fresh ginger root.....................1 tablespoon
fresh red chilli, thinly sliced....................................1
sesame oil...1 teaspoon
spring onion (scallion), to garnish

FRIED TOFU

firm tofu, cubed into 1.5 x 1.5 cm/½ x ½
    in pieces..................................about 450 g (1 lb)
sesame oil...1 teaspoon
light soy sauce...................................1 tablespoon
cornflour (cornstarch).....................4 tablespoons
salt and white pepper.............................large pinch
vegetable oil, for frying

SPICE MIX

salt...½ tablespoon
Chinese five-spice powder....................2 teaspoons
caster (superfine) sugar.......................½ tablespoon
ground white pepper..............................1 teaspoon
dried red chilli flakes (optional)............1 teaspoon

METHOD

Put the rice in a saucepan, cover with cold water, then pour off the cloudy, starchy water. Repeat three times, draining the water from the rice each time, or until the water is clear. After the final draining, return the rice to the pan and shake it from side to side so the rice levels out. Add enough cold water to the pan so that the tip of your middle finger touches the top of the rice and the water reaches your first knuckle. Bring to the boil, then reduce the heat to a simmer, put the lid on, and cook for 10–15 minutes. Once the water has fully evaporated, turn off the heat.

Preheat the oven to 160°C fan (350°F/gas 4).

Drain the tofu on paper towel to absorb the excess water for at least 10 minutes. Put the tofu in a bowl, drizzle it with the sesame oil and soy sauce, then toss. Combine the cornflour and salt and pepper in a bowl. Toss the tofu in the mix until fully coated. Pour vegetable oil into a heavy-based saucepan, wok or frying pan (skillet) to a depth of at least 1 cm (½ in) and heat over a high heat. Use the end of a wooden spoon to test the oil: once it fizzes around the handle it is ready. Fry the tofu in a couple of batches for 5 minutes until brown. Once browned, remove, put on a grill tray and keep in the warm oven to keep crisp. Pour the frying oil into a bowl for straining and reusing later.

Combine the spice mix ingredients in a bowl.

Using paper towel, strain the cooled frying oil back into the saucepan, wok or frying pan, and over a high heat add the onion, cooking for a couple of minutes. Add the pepper, garlic, ginger and chilli. Cook for a couple of minutes, then add half the salt mix and mix through the vegetables. Quickly add the crispy tofu, drizzle the sesame oil around the edge of the saucepan, wok or frying pan and toss everything together. Taste and add more of the spice mix if needed.

Cantonese-style Sweet and Sour Chicken

This recipe was the start of my 'fakeaways' series during the first lockdown. The demand for this dish was phenomenal on social media and it still is! I am still sent images each week from people making it at home. Cantonese-style sweet and sour chicken ticks so many boxes on the cravings front and it is a really easy recipe to follow.

Serves: 4
Prep: 10 minutes
Cook: 20 minutes

INGREDIENTS

CHICKEN PIECES

chicken breasts, diced	500 g (1 lb 2 oz)
salt	½ teaspoon
white pepper	½ teaspoon
large eggs, beaten	2
plain (all-purpose) flour	75 g (2½ oz/ generous ½ cup)
cornflour (cornstarch)	75 g (2½ oz/ generous ½ cup)
vegetable oil, for frying	

SWEET AND SOUR SAUCE

water	1 cup (250 ml/8 fl oz/1 cup)
caster (superfine) or granulated sugar	100 g (3½ oz/½ cup)
tomato purée	115 g (4oz)
distilled white vinegar	125 ml (4 ¼ fl oz/generous ½ cup)
cornflour (cornstarch) paste (optional)	1 tablespoon

VEGETABLES

vegetable oil	1 tablespoon
large onion, sliced	1
red (bell) pepper, deseeded and sliced into strips	1
large carrot, peeled and cut into half circles	1
large tomato, cut into wedges	1
spring onions (scallions), to garnish (optional)	

METHOD

Preheat the oven to 160°C fan (350°F/gas 4).

Season the chicken with salt and pepper. Put the eggs in a shallow bowl and combine the flour and cornflour in another shallow bowl. Dip the chicken into the beaten egg, then transfer the chicken to the flour and coat.

Pour the vegetable oil to a depth of 1 cm (½ in) in a wok or heavy-based saucepan and heat over a high heat. Use the end of a wooden spoon to test the oil. Once it fizzes around the handle it is ready. Shallow-fry the chicken pieces in batches for 5 minutes per batch until golden, drain on paper towel, then transfer to a grill rack and tray and put in the oven to keep warm and crispy.

To make the sweet and sour sauce, put the water and sugar in a saucepan and let the sugar dissolve over a low heat, then add the tomato purée and vinegar. Let the sauce bubble and keep stirring it to get rid of all the lumps, then bring to the boil to let it caramelise for a couple of minutes. Set aside.

Heat the vegetable oil in a wok or frying pan (skillet) over a high heat, add the onion and fry for a couple of minutes (add a splash of water to help soften the onions), then add the pepper, carrot and tomato wedges. Add the sauce and let it bubble away for 3–5 minutes to caramelise further. If it is not thick enough, add cornflour paste, one teaspoon at a time and letting the sauce bubble after each addition, until it reaches the desired consistency. Add the chicken pieces from the oven and toss them in the sauce and vegetables as quickly as you can, then serve right away with rice.

TOP TIP

For a healthier option, don't coat the chicken in batter.

Beef and Black Bean Sauce

Black beans are a great addition to any dish – they add a good umami kick, and can be made into a rich sauce with just a few extra ingredients. Please do not mistake Chinese black beans for Mexican black beans: they are completely different! Chinese black beans are actually soy beans which have been fermented.

Serves: 4
Prep: 10 minutes, plus minimum 15 minutes' marinating (ideally overnight)
Cook: 20 minutes

INGREDIENTS

BLACK BEAN SAUCE

dried fermented black beans (or use tinned pre-soaked black beans) .... 3 tablespoons
a little vegetable oil (if neeed)
large onion, cut into large cubes 1
grated fresh ginger root .... ½ thumb-sized piece (about 20 g/ ¾ oz)
large garlic cloves, grated 2
chicken stock cube, crumbled .... ½
large red (bell) pepper, deseeded and cut into large cubes 1
caster (superfine) sugar (optional) .... ½ teaspoon
cornflour (cornstarch) paste .... 1 tablespoon
spring onions (scallions), sliced diagonally 2
sea salt and white pepper

BEEF

beef rump steak, thinly sliced against the grain (or sirloin or fillet) .... about 500 g (1 lb 2 oz)
light soy sauce .... 1½ tablespoons
toasted sesame oil .... 1 teaspoon
cornflour (cornstarch) .... 2 teaspoons
Shaoxing wine (or mirin, white wine or water) .... 1 tablespoon
vegetable oil .... 1 tablespoon

METHOD

Put the dried fermented black beans in a small heatproof bowl, cover with boiling water and leave to soak for 15 minutes.

Put the sliced beef in a bowl with the soy sauce, sesame oil, cornflour and Shaoxing wine, stir to coat and marinate for at least 15 minutes (or in the fridge overnight).

Heat the vegetable oil for the beef in a wok or large frying pan (skillet) over a high heat, add the marinated beef and fry for a couple of minutes until it is slightly coloured but still pink – do not cook it through. Transfer to a bowl or plate.

Heat a little vegetable oil in the same pan you used for the beef, over a high heat. Add the onion cubes and a large splash of water to help them soften a little bit and cook for 2–3 minutes (the water also helps to deglaze the pan). Add the ginger and garlic, fry for about a minute until you can smell their aromas, then add the black beans (drained) and the crumbled stock cube. Fry for another minute or so, then add the pepper and the beef and 200–250 ml (7–8½ fl oz/scant 1 cup–1 cup) of water and let everything bubble away for a couple of minutes. Taste and adjust the seasoning (it should be salty enough). If it is too salty, add the sugar or more water to adjust the taste, then some cornflour paste, a teaspoon at a time, until the sauce reaches your desired thickness. Toss in the spring onions and serve with basmati rice or noodles.

TOP TIP

Fermented black beans can be bought in your local Chinese supermarket or online and are very inexpensive.

Any leftover dried or rehydrated black beans will keep in the freezer for six months.

HONG KONG WESTERN CAFÉ SPECIALS

Hong Kong is a mecca for many different cuisines, and countless signature Hong Kong dishes have made their way across the world and become super trendy.

Cha Chaan Teng is a Hong Kong Western-style café. They emerged after the Second World War in the 1950s to provide lower income households with affordable 'western' food.

I grew up with signature Hong Kong café dishes at home (and obviously when I visited Hong Kong).

My late grandparents' house in Hong Kong is in a tiny seaside village called Tai Mei Tuk; and in their courtyard, they ran a very small *Cha Chaan Teng* where travellers would have stopped by. In the late 1960s, my grandparents moved to Blackburn in the UK to seek a better life for their family, so, although they no longer have their café, there are a couple of Hong Kong cafés near their house which means I get my fix whenever I stay!

SPAM AND EGG BAP	148
HOT MILK TEA	149
ICED LEMON TEA	149
HONG KONG-STYLE FRENCH TOAST	150
SPAM AND MACARONI SOUP	152
CORNED BEEF AND EGG SANDWICH	153
MUM'S OXTAIL SOUP	156

Spam and Egg Bap

A spam – or ham – and egg sandwich is a staple in Hong Kong cafés. This is literally the first thing I would eat in the morning when I woke up in Hong Kong. There is a *Cha Chaan Teng* at the end of our ancestral home driveway in Tai Mei Tuk in Tai Po. The egg is cooked with a little bit of chicken stock powder which gives it a really yummy flavour.

My children now love this as much as I do, but we don't usually get white sliced bread or spam, so it has evolved into a ham and egg bap (which is a good old Northern Ireland bread roll!).

Serves: 2
Prep: 5 minutes
Cook: 5 minutes

INGREDIENTS

vegetable oil .... large splash
large eggs, beaten with a large pinch
   of chicken stock powder or salt 4
thin slices of spam (or ham) 6
butter, for spreading
baps 2
   or thick bread .... 4 slices

METHOD

Heat the vegetable oil in a frying pan (skillet) over a low heat, add the eggs with the chicken stock powder or salt and slowly cook them as you would an omelette: once the egg is cooked underneath and still uncooked on top, use a fork or wooden spoon and push the edges of the egg into the middle of the pan so it gathers up. This gives it a fluffy texture. Cook for a couple of minutes, but not too long as you do not want overcooked eggs. Tip out onto a plate.

In the same pan, fry the spam or ham for 2–3 minutes over a high heat until brown on both sides.

Butter the baps or bread, then put the egg and the ham or spam in the bap. We love to top it off with some ketchup!

Hot Milk Tea and Iced Lemon Tea

Hong Kong hot milk tea is like an institution, so much so that in 2017 the Leisure and Cultural Services Department of Hong Kong declared the Hong Kong-style milk tea-making technique as one of the intangible cultural heritages of Hong Kong.

This milk tea requires Lipton tea bags (the main Hong Kong tea brand). The tea bags are simmered in water for at least 5-10 minutes, depending on how strong you like your tea. The addition of condensed milk and evaporated milk gives the tea its characteristic super-creamy taste.

Cold lemon tea uses the same brewed tea but plenty of lemon which you crush with a spoon to release all the juices. The combination of the sugary, sweet and sour flavours really hits the spot when you are thirsty.

Makes: 1 drink

HOT MILK TEA

Lipton tea bags	4
condensed milk	1–2 tablespoons
evaporated milk	4–6 tablespoons

METHOD

Place the tea bags in a saucepan, pour over 600 ml (20 fl oz/2½ cups) of water and bring to the boil, then reduce to a low heat and simmer for 5–10 minutes depending on how strong you like your tea. Add the condensed milk to the bottom of a heatproof glass or mug, then pour the hot brewed tea on top, then the evaporated milk. Use a spoon to stir, then taste. Add more condensed milk if you like the tea sweeter (I love it sweet) or milkier by using more evaporated milk.

COLD LEMON TEA

Lipton tea bags	4
sugar or sweetner	1–2 teaspoons
lemon slices	at least 5
ice cubes	

METHOD

Place the tea bags in a saucepan, pour over 600 ml (20 fl oz/2½ cups) of water and bring to the boil, then reduce to a low heat and simmer for 5–10 minutes depending on how strong you like your tea. Allow the tea to cool. Put the sugar in the bottom of the glass. Add the cooled tea, lemon slices and ice. Stir well, crushing the lemon slices with the spoon to release their wonderful flavour into the tea.

TOP TIP

If you can't find Lipton yellow label tea bags use the strongest English breakfast tea bags you can find.

Hong Kong-style French Toast

This French toast is everything you want: eggy bread bursting with peanut butter and covered in condensed milk. It is usually served with a large knob of butter melting on top, but I don't think it needs it! In Hong Kong, Western cuisine was seen as sophisticated and French Toast was definitely one of those dishes that was added to the menu for a little bit of escapism for the residents of Hong Kong to enjoy!

Traditionally in Hong Kong the crusts are cut off the bread before frying, but I do not like wasting food so I usually leave the crusts intact.

Serves: 2
Prep: 10 minutes
Cook time: 5 minutes

INGREDIENTS

peanut butter (or a nut butter
    of your choice) .... 2 heaped tablespoons
thick white bread .... 4 slices
large eggs, beaten 2
butter, for frying .... 1 tablespoon
condensed milk, for drizzling

METHOD

Spread the peanut butter evenly over two of the slices of bread, then place the remaining two slices of bread on top. Put the beaten eggs in a wide, shallow bowl. Dip the peanut butter sandwiches in the beaten egg and make sure all the sides and edges are covered.

Melt the butter in a frying pan (skillet) over a medium heat, add an eggy sandwich and fry for 2–3 minutes on each side, then carefully fry the 4 edges as well, using tongs to balance it. Repeat with the other egg-dipped sandwich, then drizzle with lashings of condensed milk.

TOP TIP
This cooks very quickly, so work fast, otherwise it will burn!

Spam and Macaroni Soup

Comfort food at its best. It may seem a bit strange, but this is actually a breakfast meal in Hong Kong! A clash of cultures in Hong Kong created this pasta dish swimming in a delicious, soul-restoring chicken broth topped with ham or spam.

I add peas, carrots and sweetcorn for my children to up their veggie intake and to make it a more substantial meal.

Serves: 2
Prep: 5 minutes
Cook: 10 minutes

INGREDIENTS

salt .... large pinch
macaroni pasta tubes .... 100 g (3½ oz)
chicken stock .... 500 ml (17 fl oz/2 cups)
mixed frozen vegetables
   (carrots, sweetcorn and peas) ..... large handful
toasted sesame oil .... 2 teaspoons
light soy sauce .... 2 teaspoons
vegetable oil ....1 teaspoon
spam or ham, thinly sliced
   or chopped .... 200 g (7 oz)
sea salt and white pepper
eggs (optional)

METHOD

Bring a large saucepan of water to the boil, add a large pinch of salt, then add the pasta and cook according to the instructions on the packet, but reduce the time by at least 1 minute so the pasta is al dente. Drain the pasta and place in two bowls. Set aside.

Add the chicken stock to the saucepan, along with the vegetables, sesame oil and soy sauce, and bring to the boil. Taste and adjust for seasoning, then pour over the pasta in the serving bowls.

Heat the vegetable oil in a frying pan (skillet) over a high heat. Add the pieces of spam or ham and fry for a couple of minutes until they are lovely and crispy. Split the spam or ham between the bowls and if you want to make the soup even tastier, add a crispy fried egg!

Corned Beef and Egg Sandwich

This is a favourite ordered by many in the Hong Kong cafés. The use of corned beef came about through trade with the Commonwealth countries, and both corned beef and spam symbolise Western food.

The salty corned beef paired with soft, fluffy eggs, served in buttery crunchy toast, makes a very satisfying sandwich. You can add a splash of evaporated milk or regular milk to make the eggs even creamier.

Serves: 4
Prep: 5 minutes
Cook: 5 minutes

INGREDIENTS

tin of corned beef .... 350 g (12 oz)
large eggs 6
evaporated or regular milk (optional) .... splash
ground white pepper .... pinch
bread, toasted .... 8 slices
butter, for spreading

METHOD

Put the corned beef in a frying pan (skillet) over a medium heat (you don't need any oil as there is enough in the corned beef) and heat through to break it down into pieces, allowing it to sizzle.

Beat the eggs in a bowl and add a splash of evaporated or regular milk (if using) and the white pepper. Pour the mixture over the corned beef, reduce the heat and cook the eggs slowly for a couple of minutes, using a fork or wooden spoon to push the edges of the egg and corned beef mixture into the middle of the pan so it gathers together. Be careful not to overcook the eggs.

Toast and butter the bread, then pile on the egg and corned beef mixture, and enjoy!

Spam and
Macaroni Soup 152

Corned Beef and
Egg Sandwich 153

Mum's Oxtail Soup

My mum used to make this soup and it's one you will want to keep going back to for more. Known as *lo sung tong* (Russian soup), this dish made its way to Hong Kong in the 1920s. This recipe makes a very large pot of soup, but you cannot help but have more than one serving, so it doesn't last long.

Serves: 8
Prep: 15 minutes
Cook: 2 hours

INGREDIENTS

beef oxtail or ribs .... about 750 g (1 lb 10 oz)
vegetable oil .... 2 tablespoons
large onion, roughly diced 1
medium carrots, peeled and cut into chunks 2
large celery sticks, cut into chunks 2
large garlic cloves, crushed 6
large tomatoes, sliced 4
tin of chopped tomatoes .... 400 g (14 oz)
caster (superfine) sugar .... 2 teaspoons
small white cabbage,
    cut into chunks ....1 (about 600 g/1 lb 5 oz)
bay leaves 3
tomato purée .... 4 tablespoons
Worcestershire sauce .... 3 tablespoons
paprika .... 3 teaspoons
chicken or beef stock (I use
    the broth from boiling
    the oxtail/ribs) .... 1.5 litres
                                    (50 fl oz/6¼ cups)
large white potatoes, peeled,
    chopped and cubed 2
sea salt and white pepper
cornflour (cornstarch) paste

METHOD

Put the oxtail or beef ribs in a stock pot, cover with water (so it sits at least 5 cm/2 in above the meat), then bring to the boil and cook for 10 minutes, scooping off any scum from the surface with a large spoon. Drain the oxtail or ribs and set aside (reserving the beef broth to use later instead of the beef or chicken stock, if you wish).

Heat the oil in a large saucepan (or use another stock pot if you have one) over a high heat, add the onion, carrots, celery and garlic, and fry for 5 minutes until the garlic starts to become fragrant, making sure the other vegetables do not burn – if necessary, add a splash of water. Add the fresh tomatoes, tinned tomatoes, sugar, cabbage, bay leaves, tomato purée, Worcestershire sauce and paprika, then the oxtail or beef ribs. Add the stock or beef broth left over from boiling the oxtail or beef ribs, then bring everything to the boil and simmer for 45 minutes. Add the potatoes and simmer for a further 30 minutes or until soft. Taste and season with salt and pepper, and if you would like a sharper or tangier flavour, add more Worcestershire sauce. This soup is ready after 1 hour and 15 minutes, but I prefer to simmer it for at least another 30 minutes or so, until the meat is really tender.

TOP TIP

This soup tastes even better the next day if you can resist eating it at one sitting.

BREAD AND SWEETS

Trying to choose which of my favourite Chinese sweet and bread dishes I would feature in this chapter was super difficult, but I was guided by my little ones, so here are our top five! The Chinese milk bread is such a versatile one and is the base bread for pineapple buns, frankfurter buns and coconut buns. The *dan tat* and mango puddings are classics from dim sum and just a must on your to-try list. The cookies and sesame bars are just great snacks that keep well in a sealed container (but never really make it past day two in our house!).

CHAPTER ELEVEN

CHINESE MILK BREAD	160
DAN TAT	162
MANGO PUDDING	164
ALMOND AND PEANUT COOKIES	166
BLACK AND WHITE SESAME BARS	168

Chinese Milk Bread

Milk bread is one of those soft breads that, like brioche, once you start eating it, you can't stop. The dough involves making a milk roux paste, which is combined with flour, sugar, condensed milk and butter to make the dough. The paste is also the base for a huge variety of Chinese breads, such as pineapple bread and coconut swirl bread.

Makes: 1 loaf
Prep: 30 minutes, plus 2 hours' proving time
Cook: 30–40 minutes

INGREDIENTS

yeast .... 8 g (⅓ oz)
lukewarm milk, plus extra for
    brushing ..... 125 ml (4¼ fl oz/generous ½ cup)

ROUX

plain flour .... 2½ tablespoons
whole milk .... 65 ml (2 fl oz/¼ cup)
water .... 55 ml (1¾ fl oz/3½ tablespoons)

DOUGH

plain (all-purpose) flour .... 350 g (12 oz/2¾ cups)
caster (superfine)
    sugar .... 35 g (1¼ oz/3 tablespoons)
salt .... 3 g
medium egg 1
condensed milk .... 40 g (1½ oz)
butter, melted, plus extra
    for greasing .... 60 g (2¼ oz)

SUGAR SYRUP

caster (superfine) sugar .... 50 g (1¾ oz/ ¼ cup)
boiling water .... 50 ml (1¾ fl oz/3½ tablespoons)

METHOD

Add the yeast to the lukewarm milk and stir it in so it 'blooms' (the surface will go foamy, which means the yeast is working).

To make the dough, follow the instructions for *Bread Dough* on page 12.

Punch down the risen dough and divide it into as many portions as you would like. Make sure you tuck in the sides of the rolls. Butter a 900 g (2 lb) loaf tin (pan). Line the rolls in next to each other in the greased tin and cover again. Leave the tin for 30–40 minutes in a warm place until the bread has doubled in size.

Preheat the oven to 160°C fan (350°F/gas 4). Brush the top of the rolls with milk, being careful not to let it drip down the sides too much, otherwise the bread will stick to the tin. Bake on the bottom shelf of the oven for 30–40 minutes until golden brown.

While the bread is in the oven, make a sugar syrup by dissolving the sugar in the water and allowing to cool. As soon as you remove the bread from the oven, immediately brush it all over with the syrup.

TOP TIP

Letting the dough sit once all the ingredients are mixed together really helps to develop the gluten and also makes the dough easier to knead if you do not have a mixer.

Dan Tat

Dan tat is the classic Cantonese egg tart, which was influenced by the British shortcrust egg tarts. However, the Hong Kong versions are made with a flaky water pastry and the filling is made from eggs and evaporated milk. I love these – they were such massive treats at dim sum and I remember squabbling with my siblings over who would get one.

Makes: 16 tarts
Prep: 30 minutes, plus chilling time (preferably overnight for the pastry)
Cook: 20 minutes

INGREDIENTS

BUTTER CRUMB

plain (all-purpose) flour .... 100 g (3½ oz/¾ cup)
frozen butter, grated (keep it in the
    freezer until you need it) .... 150 g (5 oz)

WATER PASTRY

plain (all-purpose) flour .... 200 g (7 oz/1⅔ cups)
icing (confectioner's) sugar,
    sifted .... 50 g (1¾ oz/generous ⅓ cup)
small egg 1
vegetable oil, for greasing

EGG FILLING

icing (confectioner's)
    sugar .... 75 g (2½ oz/generous ½ cup)
medium eggs 5
evaporated milk .... 120 g (4¼ oz)
vanilla extract .... 1 teaspoon

METHOD

To make the butter crumb and water pastry, follow the instructions on page 12.

To make the egg filling, dissolve the icing sugar in 160 ml (5½ fl oz/⅔ cup) of hot water in a bowl, then whisk in the eggs, evaporated milk and vanilla extract, strain through a fine sieve into a jug, cover and place in the fridge.

Roll out the dough between the two pieces of cling film (plastic wrap) in which it is wrapped, to a thickness of 2–3 mm (1⁄16–⅛ in), then cut into 16 discs with a 12 cm (5 in) fluted cutter and place each disc in 8 cm (3 in) fluted tins (pans). Use your fingers to gently push the pastry into the bottom and sides, but not the top edges, of each tin – be careful not to squash the pastry, otherwise it will not puff and flake up. Trim the loose ragged edges with a sharp knife and put the individual tins in a sturdy baking tray (pan). Place in the fridge for 5–10 minutes to harden (they bake the best after an overnight chill).

Preheat the oven to 180°C fan (400°F/gas 6), placing a heavy-duty baking tray turned upside down on the middle shelf. The dan tats will sit on this surface, which ensures the bases crisp up and don't become soggy!

Pour the egg mixture into the pastry shells so they are about 70 per cent full. Transfer carefully to the oven and bake (on top of the upside-down heated baking tray) for 10 minutes, then reduce the heat to 140°C fan (325°F/gas 3) and bake for a further 10 minutes. If the egg mixture starts to rise and puff in the middle, open the oven door for about 15 seconds, then close it again. The middle of the tarts should be slightly wobbly and will set after sitting for 5 minutes. Leave in the tins for about 10 minutes before you try to remove them from the tins. Enjoy!

BREAD AND SWEETS

Mango Pudding

In Hong Kong there are many dessert houses that specialise in fruit-based desserts. One of my favourite desserts is mango pudding. This dessert is usually presented as a perfectly set, freestanding jelly, but I wanted to reproduce this as fuss-free as possible, so you don't need to worry about it setting and therefore turning it out!

Serves: 6
Prep: 5 minutes,
plus minimum
4 hours' chilling time

INGREDIENTS

caster (superfine) sugar ....75 g (2½ oz/⅓ cup)
gelatine powder ....1 heaped tablespoon
vanilla extract ....1 teaspoon
evaporated milk, plus extra
    to serve ....350 ml (12 fl oz/1½ cups)
tinned mango purée, plus extra
    to serve ....350 ml (12 fl oz/1½ cups)
freshly cut mango chunks, to serve

METHOD

Pour 150 ml (5 fl oz/scant ⅔ cup) boiling water into a large, 1-litre (34 fl oz/4 cup) measuring jug, add the sugar and the gelatine powder, and stir to dissolve. Add the vanilla extract, evaporated milk and mango purée, and pulse with a handheld blender until everything is super smooth. Pour the mixture through a sieve into a clean bowl or jug to remove any bits, then divide among six glasses or ramekins. Cover with cling film (plastic wrap) and leave in the fridge for at least 4 hours or overnight.

Once you are ready to serve, add a layer of evaporated milk and drizzle over some mango purée. Add mango chunks to serve.

Almond and Peanut Cookies

The almond cookie is a crumbly and very moreish Chinese New Year treat. The cookies date back to the 16th century and are said to bring good fortune. I wanted to give these more crunch, so I added some roasted peanuts and it was a triumph – my taste-tester children definitely approve.

Makes: about 18 cookies
Prep: 10 minutes
Cook: 12 minutes

INGREDIENTS

cold butter, grated .... 100 g (3½ oz)
plain (all-purpose) flour .... 125 g (4¼ oz/1¼ cups)
bicarbonate of soda (baking soda) .... ¼ teaspoon
ground almonds
   (almond meal) .... 125 g (4¼ oz/1¼ cups)
granulated sugar .... 100 g (3½ oz/scant ½ cup)
small egg, beaten 1
almond extract .... 1½ teaspoons
toasted unsalted peanuts,
   roughly chopped .... 50 g (1¾ oz)
whole almonds, for topping .... about 18
egg, beaten, for glazing 1

METHOD

Preheat the oven to 160°C fan (350°F/gas 4) and line two baking trays (pans) with baking parchment.

Put the cold grated butter in a bowl, add the flour and bicarbonate of soda and rub the mixture with your fingertips until it resembles breadcrumbs. Stir in the ground almonds and sugar, then add the egg, almond extract and peanuts, and mix well with a knife or wooden spoon until you have a stiff dough.

Divide the dough into 18 even-sized pieces then roll into balls and space out evenly on the two baking trays (the cookies will spread a little, so do not put them too close together). Use the palm of your hand to flatten them down slightly. Place one almond on top of each cookie and glaze with the beaten egg.

Bake in the oven for about 12 minutes until golden. Remove from the oven and leave on the trays for about 10 minutes to harden, otherwise they will fall apart; they are a very crumbly cookie.

TOP TIP

Do not overwork the butter with your hands as it will melt. If this happens, put the cookies in the fridge for at least 15 minutes before baking, so they can harden up.

Black and White Sesame Bars

Sesame brittle is one of those amazing treats that is just so addictive. These bars are made with two different types of sesame seeds and peanuts, and they really hit the spot. If you are craving a treat, this is a great one to pick up as it is high in protein.

Makes: 12 bars
Prep: 10 minutes, plus 1 hour cooling
Cook: 10–15 minutes

INGREDIENTS

skinless unsalted peanuts .... 200 g (7 oz)
white sesame seeds .... 100 g (3½ oz)
black sesame seeds .... 100 g (3½ oz)
granulated sugar .... 325 g (11½ oz/1½ cups plus 2 tablespoons)
butter, melted .... 50 g (1¾ oz)

METHOD

Line a 20-cm (8-in) square baking tray (pan) with baking parchment.

Toast all the peanuts and both types of sesame seeds in a dry frying pan (skillet) over a low to medium heat for a couple of minutes (make sure you don't burn them), then tip out into a dish.

Wipe clean the pan (make sure it is super clean), then add the sugar. Spread the sugar out flat with the palm of your hand, then place the pan over a low heat. Once the edges of the sugar have melted and turned golden, the rest of the caramel will form very quickly – tip the pan from side to side, so the caramel colours evenly and all the granules melt. Do not stick in a spoon to stir: it will immediately crystallise the caramel and ruin it. The caramel will take about 10 minutes to melt and turn golden: be patient!

Quickly add the melted butter and stir with a spatula until you have a toffee sauce (this takes seconds of stirring, so be ready to add in the rest of the ingredients). Add the peanuts and sesame seeds, quickly stir, and tip into the lined tray. Press down with another piece of baking parchment, so the mixture is evenly spread out. Mark 12 bars on top of the slab, so they are easier to snap apart when set.

Leave to cool completely (this will take about an hour), then cut with a sharp knife to the desired 'bar size'. The bars will keep in an airtight container for up to two weeks, but they never make it to the end of the week for us!

TOP TIP

The bars can be made with hazelnuts, almonds or any other nut you have to hand. Just make sure you toast them first, as this really enhances the flavour!

ABOUT THE AUTHOR AND ACKNOWLEDGEMENTS

Suzie Lee is a Chinese cook, the 2020 winner of BBC's *Best Home Cook* and the presenter of *Suzie Lee Home Cook Hero*. Brought up by her Hong Kong parents in Northern Ireland, Suzie was taught to cook by her mum Celia, who sadly passed away when she was just 16. Even before winning *Best Home Cook*, Suzie was always being asked for her recipes and top tips in the kitchen. She believes that cooking should be fun, simple and loved by all, and so, in this book, has included recipes that are firm family favourites and can be made by people of all skill levels. Suzie gives demonstrations at a range of regional and national food shows around the UK and has worked with a leading supermarket in Northern Ireland to develop a range of brand-new ready meals.

I really have a list as long as my arm in terms of who I would like to thank ... but I am going to give it a go.

Firstly, I would like to thank my mum, Celia, who unfortunately is no longer with us. She is my inspiration in all areas of life and, most importantly, passed on to me her love of food. She is the woman who gave me my grit and determination to do my very best in everything. Thank you, Mum, this book is for you!

My husband, Stevie, who since 2001 has been the Yin to my Yang, the voice of reason in my doubtful moments of despair, and 'my person' who just kicks me up the backside when I need it! He has been there to push and support me when no one else was about.

My two little rascals, Zander and Odie, for eating everything I put in front of them. They were tough critics to please sometimes, but their favourite chapter had to be the dumplings and dim sum.

My siblings, Angela, Winnie, Veronica and Timmy, who all had an input in this book. My dad, Peter, for helping me to remember Mum's dishes and who was a sounding board for some of the recipes.

My sister-in-law, Kirsty Lee, thank you for keeping me right in Chinese food etiquette and bouncing off ideas with me for recipes.

My top food testers, Jonny Baxter, Jill Caskey and Odhran Devlin, your honest opinions were very welcomed.

Anne Kibel, who took a chance on me and became my wonderful agent. She told me to focus on the special USP of my ethnicity ... if she had not pushed me on this, I would not have created this cookbook at all. She believed in me and here we are!

Lynne and Ivan (my in-laws) and Elizabeth Ramsey who have helped me on countless occasions with my little ones when I needed to get into the right headspace to keep developing/writing/retesting my recipes. Thank you from the bottom of my heart!

The Hardie Grant crew of Kajal Mistry and Kate Burkett, thank you for having the confidence in me and publishing this cookbook. Lizzie Mayson, Kitty Coles, Florence Blair and Hattie Baker for making it all come alive; the book is just beautiful and it is better than I could ever have imagined!

INDEX

A

almond and peanut cookies 166
asparagus: beef, black pepper and
asparagus 103
aubergines
    ma po tofu with aubergine 106
    stuffed aubergines with black
      bean sauce 52

B

bamboo shoots
    hot and sour soup 137
    mixed veg stir-fry with bamboo
      shoots and water chestnuts 51
    prawn dumplings 61
    veggie spring rolls 132–3
bao buns 11
sticky pork belly bao buns with
  Suzie's pickled vegetables 72
baozi dough 11
sausage meat and spring onion
  dumplings 70
baps: spam and egg bap 148
beansprouts
    beef *ho fun* noodles 114
    veggie spring rolls 132–3
beef. *see also* steak
    beef and black bean sauce 144
    beef, black pepper and
      asparagus 103
    beef *ho fun* noodles 114
    Chinese beef brisket 90
    ma po tofu with aubergine 106
    mum's oxtail soup 156
black beans
    beef and black bean sauce 144
    Cantonese steamed black
      bean, ginger and spring
      onion salmon 126
    stuffed aubergines with black
      bean sauce 52
black pepper sauce: beef, black
  pepper and asparagus 103
bread. *see also* baps; sandwiches;
  toast
    bread dough 12
    Chinese milk bread 160
butter crumb 12
butternut squash: stewed pork
  ribs with potatoes and butternut
  squash 92

C

cabbage
    Chinese cabbage and shiitake
      mushrooms 46
    XO sauce udon noodles 128
carrots
    Chinese beef brisket 90
    crispy seafood noodles 82
    king prawns, celery and carrot 123
    XO sauce udon noodles 128
cashew nuts
    king prawns, celery and carrot 123
    quorn and cashew nut stir-fry 95
celery: king prawns, celery and
  carrot 123
chicken
    Cantonese-style sweet and sour
      chicken 143
    char siu chicken fillets 96
    chicken and sweetcorn soup 138
    chicken congee with deep-fried
      savoury donut sticks 67
    Hainanese chicken rice 26
    Hong Kong style chicken
      wings 117
    hot and sour soup 137
    soy sauce chicken 20
    Suzie's Chinese fried chicken 22
    yin yang fried rice 76
chilli oil: spicy crispy tofu bites with
  Suzie's chilli oil 48
chillies
    deep-fried fish cakes with tangy
      dipping sauce 37
    ma po tofu with aubergine 106
    mixed veg stir-fry with bamboo
      shoots and water chestnuts 51
    salted chilli tofu with perfect
      basmati rice 140
    turkey pot stickers 68
    veggie spring rolls 132–3
Chinese cabbage and shiitake
  mushrooms 46
Chinese five spice
    char siu chicken fillets 96
    Chinese beef brisket 90
    crispy pork belly 16–17
    duck pancakes 18
    Peking pork chops 25
    salted chilli tofu with perfect
      basmati rice 140
    spicy crispy tofu bites with
      Suzie's chilli oil 48
    Suzie's Chinese fried chicken 22
    tea eggs 121

Chinese leaf: homemade wonton
  soup noodles 78
condensed milk
    Chinese milk bread 160
    Hong Kong-style French toast 150
    hot milk tea 149
cookies: almond and peanut
  cookies 166
corned beef and egg sandwich 153
cornflour 9
courgettes: quorn and cashew nut
  stir-fry 95
cucumber
    duck pancakes 18
    sticky pork belly bao buns with
      Suzie's pickled vegetables 72
curry powder: veggie Singapore
  noodles 84

D

dim sum
    chicken congee with deep-fried
      savoury donut sticks 67
    sticky pork belly bao buns with
      Suzie's pickled vegetables 72
dipping sauce
    turkey pot stickers 68
    veggie spring rolls 132–3
donut dough 10
    chicken congee with deep-fried
      savoury donut sticks 67
dough 10–13
duck
    duck and pineapple fried rice 86
    duck pancakes 18
dumplings
    pork and prawn dumplings 62
    prawn dumplings 61
    sausage meat and spring onion
      dumplings 70
    turkey pot stickers 68

E

egg noodles 11–12
eggs
    char siu, green bean and
      egg hash 111
    corned beef and egg
      sandwich 153
    dan tat 162

egg and tomato 104
Hong Kong-style French
   toast 150
instant noodle bowl 118
spam and egg bap 148
steamed eggs 94
tea eggs 121
veggie Singapore noodles 84
yin yang fried rice 76
equipment 8
evaporated milk
   dan tat 162
   hot milk tea 149
   mango pudding 164

F

fish
   classic Hong Kong-style steamed
      whole fish 34
   crispy fish with sweetcorn
      sauce 42
   deep-fried fish cakes with tangy
      dipping sauce 37
frankfurters: ketchup
   frankfurters 100

G

garlic
   beef and black bean sauce 144
   beef, black pepper and
      asparagus 103
   beef *ho fun* noodles 114
   Cantonese steamed black
      bean, ginger and spring onion
      salmon 126
   Chinese cabbage and shiitake
      mushrooms 46
   crispy fish with sweetcorn sauce 42
   crispy seafood noodles 82
   deep-fried fish cakes with tangy
      dipping sauce 37
   duck and pineapple fried rice 86
   garlic mixed mushrooms 54
   garlicky scallops on glass
      noodles 38
   Hainanese chicken rice 26
   homemade wonton soup
      noodles 78
   Hong Kong style chicken
      wings 117
   hot and sour soup 137
   instant noodle bowl 118
   king prawns, celery and
      carrot 123
   ma po tofu with aubergine 106
   mixed veg stir-fry with bamboo
      shoots and water chestnuts 51
   mixed veggie egg-fried rice 124
   mum's oxtail soup 156
   quorn and cashew nut stir-fry 95
   salted chilli tofu with perfect
      basmati rice 140
   spicy crispy tofu bites with
      Suzie's chilli oil 48

stewed pork ribs with potatoes
   and butternut squash 92
sticky pork belly bao buns with
   Suzie's pickled vegetables 72
Suzie's Chinese fried chicken 22
sweet and spicy king prawns 32
tofu puff stir-fry 56
turkey pot stickers 68
veggie Singapore noodles 84
veggie spring rolls 132–3
ginger
   beef and black bean sauce 144
   beef *ho fun* noodles 114
   Cantonese steamed black
      bean, ginger and spring
      onion salmon 126
   chicken congee with deep-fried
      savoury donut sticks 67
   Chinese beef brisket 90
   Chinese cabbage and shiitake
      mushrooms 46
   classic Hong Kong-style steamed
      whole fish 34
   crispy seafood noodles 82
   duck and pineapple fried rice 86
   duck pancakes 18
   ginger and spring onion
      mussels 40
   Hainanese chicken rice 26
   homemade wonton soup
      noodles 78
   hot and sour soup 137
   king prawn sesame toast 134
   ma po tofu with aubergine 106
   mixed veg stir-fry with bamboo
      shoots and water chestnuts 51
   mixed veggie egg-fried rice 124
   pork and prawn dumplings 62
   prawn dumplings 61
   salted chilli tofu with perfect
      basmati rice 140
   sausage meat and spring onion
      dumplings 70
   soy sauce chicken 20
   stewed pork ribs with potatoes
      and butternut squash 92
   sticky pork belly bao buns with
      Suzie's pickled vegetables 72
   stuffed aubergines with black
      bean sauce 52
   Suzie's Chinese fried chicken 22
   sweet and spicy king prawns 32
   tea eggs 121
   tofu puff stir-fry 56
   turkey pot stickers 68
   veggie spring rolls 132–3
green beans: *char siu*, green bean
   and egg hash 111
greens: Chinese cabbage and
   shiitake mushrooms 46
gyoza wrapper dough 10–11
   turkey pot stickers 68

H

ham: hot and sour soup 137
hoisin sauce

char siu chicken fillets 96
cheung fun noodle bowl 81
duck pancakes 18
Peking pork chops 25
spicy crispy tofu bites with
   Suzie's chilli oil 48

I

ingredients 7–8

L

lager: ginger and spring onion
   mussels 40
lemons: cold lemon tea 149
lily flowers: garlic mixed
   mushrooms 54

M

macaroni: spam and macaroni
   soup 152
mango pudding 164
menu plans 43, 50
milk: Chinese milk bread 160
mushrooms
   Chinese cabbage and shiitake
      mushrooms 46
   crispy seafood noodles 82
   garlic mixed mushrooms 54
   hot and sour soup 137
   pork and prawn dumplings 62
   stuffed aubergines with black
      bean sauce 52
   tofu puff stir-fry 56
   turkey pot stickers 68
   veggie spring rolls 132–3
   XO sauce udon noodles 128
mussels: ginger and spring onion
   mussels 40

N

noodles
   beef *ho fun* noodles 114
   cheung fun noodle bowl 81
   cold sesame and peanut
      noodles 108
   crispy seafood noodles 82
   egg noodles 11–12
   garlicky scallops on glass
      noodles 38
   homemade wonton soup
      noodles 78
   instant noodle bowl 118
   veggie Singapore noodles 84
   XO sauce udon noodles 128

O

oyster sauce
beef, black pepper and
asparagus 103
char siu chicken fillets 96
chicken congee with deep-fried
savoury donut sticks 67
Chinese beef brisket 90
Chinese cabbage and shiitake
mushrooms 46
crispy seafood noodles 82
duck and pineapple fried rice 86
garlic mixed mushrooms 54
ginger and spring onion
mussels 40
king prawns, celery and carrot 123
mixed veg stir-fry with bamboo
shoots and water chestnuts 51
mixed veggie egg-fried rice 124
pork and prawn dumplings 62
prawn dumplings 61
quorn and cashew nut stir-fry 95
tofu puff stir-fry 56
XO sauce udon noodles 128

P

pak choi: garlic mixed mushrooms 54
pancakes
duck pancakes 18
pancake wrappers 10
pastry 12–13
peanut butter
cheung fun noodle bowl 81
cold sesame and peanut
noodles 108
Hong Kong-style French toast 150
peanuts
almond and peanut cookies 166
black and white sesame bars 168
cold sesame and peanut
noodles 108
peas
crispy fish with sweetcorn
sauce 42
duck and pineapple fried rice 86
yin yang fried rice 76
peppers
beef and black bean sauce 144
quorn and cashew nut stir-fry 95
salted chilli tofu with perfect
basmati rice 140
pineapple: duck and pineapple
fried rice 86
pork
char siu, green bean and egg
hash 111
crispy pork belly 16–17
homemade wonton soup
noodles 78
Peking pork chops 25
pork and prawn dumplings 62
sausage meat and spring onion
dumplings 70
stewed pork ribs with potatoes
and butternut squash 92
sticky pork belly bao buns with

Suzie's pickled vegetables 72
potatoes: stewed pork ribs with
potatoes and butternut squash 92
prawns
crispy seafood noodles 82
homemade wonton soup
noodles 78
king prawn sesame toast 134
king prawns, celery and
carrot 123
pork and prawn dumplings 62
prawn dumplings 61
sweet and spicy king prawns 32
yin yang fried rice 76

Q

quorn mince
quorn and cashew nut stir-fry 95
stuffed aubergines with black
bean sauce 52

R

red sauce: yin yang fried rice 76
rice
chicken congee with deep-fried
savoury donut sticks 67
duck and pineapple fried rice 86
Hainanese chicken rice 26
mixed veggie egg-fried rice 124
salted chilli tofu with perfect
basmati rice 140
yin yang fried rice 76
rice wine vinegar
cold sesame and peanut
noodles 108
deep-fried fish cakes with tangy
dipping sauce 37
sticky pork belly bao buns with
Suzie's pickled vegetables 72
sweet and spicy king prawns 32

S

salmon: Cantonese steamed black
bean, ginger and spring onion
salmon 126
sandwiches
corned beef and egg
sandwich 153
spam and egg bap 148
sausage meat and spring onion
dumplings 70
scallops
garlicky scallops on glass
noodles 38
king prawns, celery and
carrot 123
sea bream: classic Hong Kong-style
steamed whole fish 34
sesame seeds
black and white sesame bars 168
cheung fun noodle bowl 81

cold sesame and peanut
noodles 108
ketchup frankfurters 100
king prawn sesame toast 134
spicy crispy tofu bites with
Suzie's chilli oil 48
Shaoxing wine
beef and black bean sauce 144
beef, black pepper and
asparagus 103
beef *ho fun* noodles 114
Chinese beef brisket 90
crispy seafood noodles 82
duck and pineapple fried rice 86
garlic mixed mushrooms 54
homemade wonton soup
noodles 78
king prawns, celery and
carrot 123
mixed veg stir-fry with bamboo
shoots and water chestnuts 51
Peking pork chops 25
pork and prawn dumplings 62
soy sauce chicken 20
stewed pork ribs with potatoes
and butternut squash 92
sweet and spicy king prawns 32
tea eggs 121
soup
chicken and sweetcorn soup 138
homemade wonton soup
noodles 78
hot and sour soup 137
mum's oxtail soup 156
spam and macaroni soup 152
soy sauce
beef and black bean sauce 144
beef, black pepper and
asparagus 103
beef *ho fun* noodles 114
Cantonese steamed black
bean, ginger and spring
onion salmon 126
char siu chicken fillets 96
char siu, green bean and egg
hash 111
cheung fun noodle bowl 81
chicken congee with deep-fried
savoury donut sticks 67
Chinese beef brisket 90
Chinese cabbage and shiitake
mushrooms 46
classic Hong Kong-style steamed
whole fish 34
cold sesame and peanut
noodles 108
duck and pineapple fried rice 86
garlicky scallops on glass
noodles 38
ginger and spring onion
mussels 40
grandad's special steak 28
homemade wonton soup
noodles 78
Hong Kong style chicken
wings 117
hot and sour soup 137
instant noodle bowl 118
mixed veggie egg-fried rice 124
Peking pork chops 25

pork and prawn dumplings 62
quorn and cashew nut stir-fry 95
salted chilli tofu with perfect
basmati rice 140
sausage meat and spring onion
dumplings 70
soy sauce chicken 20
spam and macaroni soup 152
spicy crispy tofu bites with
Suzie's chilli oil 48
steamed eggs 94
stewed pork ribs with potatoes
and butternut squash 92
sticky pork belly bao buns with
Suzie's pickled vegetables 72
stuffed aubergines with black
bean sauce 52
Suzie's Chinese fried chicken 22
tea eggs 121
tofu puff stir-fry 56
turkey pot stickers 68
veggie Singapore noodles 84
veggie spring rolls 132–3
XO sauce udon noodles 128
spam
spam and egg bap 148
spam and macaroni soup 152
spring onions
beef *ho fun* noodles 114
Cantonese steamed black
bean, ginger and spring
onion salmon 126
cheung fun noodle bowl 81
Chinese beef brisket 90
classic Hong Kong-style steamed
whole fish 34
crispy seafood noodles 82
deep-fried fish cakes with tangy
dipping sauce 37
duck pancakes 18
garlicky scallops on glass
noodles 38
ginger and spring onion
mussels 40
Hainanese chicken rice 26
homemade wonton soup
noodles 78
pork and prawn dumplings 62
sausage meat and spring onion
dumplings 70
soy sauce chicken 20
steamed eggs 94
stewed pork ribs with potatoes
and butternut squash 92
sweet and spicy king prawns 32
turkey pot stickers 68
veggie Singapore noodles 84
spring roll wrapper 12
spring rolls: veggie spring rolls 132–3
squid
crispy seafood noodles 82
deep-fried fish cakes with tangy
dipping sauce 37
star anise
Chinese beef brisket 90
soy sauce chicken 20
tea eggs 121
steak
beef, black pepper and
asparagus 103

grandad's special steak 28
sweet & sour sauce: Cantonese-
style sweet and sour chicken 143
sweetcorn
chicken and sweetcorn soup 138
crispy fish with sweetcorn
sauce 42

T

tahini: cold sesame and peanut
noodles 108
tarts: *dan tat* 162
tea 149
cold lemon tea 149
hot milk tea 149
tea eggs 121
toast
Hong Kong-style French
toast 150
king prawn sesame toast 134
tofu
hot and sour soup 137
ma po tofu with aubergine 106
salted chilli tofu with perfect
basmati rice 140
spicy crispy tofu bites with
Suzie's chilli oil 48
tofu puff stir-fry 56
tomato ketchup
egg and tomato 104
ketchup frankfurters 100
Peking pork chops 25
sweet and spicy king prawns 32
yin yang fried rice 76
tomatoes
egg and tomato 104
mum's oxtail soup 156
yin yang fried rice 76
treacle: *char siu* chicken fillets 96
turkey pot stickers 68

V

vegetables
Cantonese-style sweet and
sour chicken 143
cold sesame and peanut
noodles 108
instant noodle bowl 118
mixed veg stir-fry with bamboo
shoots and water chestnuts 51
mixed veggie egg-fried rice 124
mum's oxtail soup 156
spam and macaroni soup 152
sticky pork belly bao buns with
Suzie's pickled vegetables 72
tofu puff stir-fry 56
veggie Singapore noodles 84
veggie spring rolls 132–3
XO sauce udon noodles 128

W

water chestnuts: mixed veg stir-fry
with bamboo shoots and water
chestnuts 51
white sauce: yin yang fried rice 76
wonton wrappers 11–12
Worcestershire sauce
grandad's special steak 28
mum's oxtail soup 156
Peking pork chops 25
wrappers 10–12. *see also* dumplings

X

XO sauce
garlicky scallops on glass
noodles 38
XO sauce udon noodles 128

175

Published in 2022 by Hardie Grant Books,
an imprint of Hardie Grant Publishing

Hardie Grant Books (London)
5th & 6th Floors
52–54 Southwark Street
London SE1 1UN

Hardie Grant Books (Melbourne)
Building 1, 658 Church Street
Richmond, Victoria 3121

hardiegrantbooks.com

All rights reserved. No part of this publication
may be reproduced, stored in a retrieval system
or transmitted in any form by any means, electronic,
mechanical, photocopying, recording or otherwise,
without the prior written permission of the publishers
and copyright holders.

The moral rights of the author have been asserted.

Copyright text © Suzie Lee
Copyright photography © Lizzie Mayson

British Library Cataloguing-in-Publication Data.
A catalogue record for this book is available from
the British Library.

Simply Chinese
ISBN: 9-781-78488-533-5

10 9 8 7 6 5 4 3 2

Publishing Director and Commissioning Editor: Kajal Mistry
Project Editor: Kate Burkett
Design and Illustrations: Evi-O. Studio | Susan Le, Wilson Leung and Katherine Zhang
Photographer: Lizzie Mayson
Food and Prop Stylist: Kitty Coles
Photography Assistant: Matthew Hague and Ollie Grove
Food Assistants: Florence Blair and Hattie Baker
Copy Editor: Laura Nickoll
Proofreader: Caroline West
Indexer: Cathy Heath
Production Controller: Lisa Fiske

Colour reproduction by p2d

Printed and bound in China by Leo Paper Products Ltd.

FSC
www.fsc.org

MIX
Paper from
responsible sources
FSC™ C020056

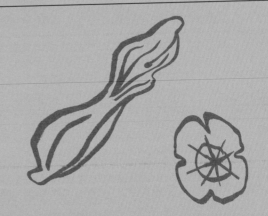